To Donn F. Draeger
who showed us the way

Marishiten, the warrior goddess, from a mid-Edo period Jigen-ryu scroll.
Tom Dreitlein Collection.

Koryu Bujutsu

Classical Warrior Traditions of Japan

**Edited by
Diane Skoss**

**Koryu Books
Warren, New Jersey**

Published by Koryu Books
P.O. Box 4464
Warren, New Jersey
www.koryu.com

First printed 1997
Third printing 2014
Book and cover design by Koryu Books
Printed in the United States of America

Cover photo of Kobayashi Masao demonstrating Shingyoto-ryu nitto kenjutsu
at Meiji Shrine ©1995 Inoue Kazuhiro.
Frontispiece courtesy Tom Dreitlein.
Photos on pages 62, 64, 68, 70, 72, 74, 76, 78, 80, 84 (top) & 134
©1995 Inoue Kazuhiro. Used with permission of the photographer.
Photo on page 57 ©1997 Eric Montes. Used with permission.
Photos on pages 89, 104, 105, & 109 courtesy David A. Hall.
Photos on pages 146, 151, & 153 courtesy Kato Takashi.
Photo on page 149 courtesy Liam Keeley.
All other photos are from the collection of Meik and Diane Skoss.

Publisher's Cataloging-in-Publication
(Provided by Quality Books, Inc.)

Koryu bujutsu : classical warrior traditions of Japan / edited by
    Diane Skoss.
        p. cm.
        ISBN: 978-1-890536-04-6
        Includes bibliographical references (p.) and index.

    1. Martial arts—Japan. 2. Martial arts—Training—
Psychological aspects. 3. Martial arts—Religious
aspects—Buddhism. I. Skoss, Diane.

GV1100.77.A2K67 1997
796.8'0952

CONTENTS

FOREWORD

I have been a United States Marine for my entire adult life. Both as an enlisted man and now as an officer of Marines, my primary goal has been to be ready to go into harm's way. The physical and mental mindset that galvanizes this calling can be found within the teachings of the *koryu bujutsu*. As a young Marine, I read the legendary Donn F. Draeger's books about the classical bujutsu and dreamt of flashing *naginata* and deep secrets obtained from mystic masters. At the same time, I was reading the fabulous history of the Marine Corps and envisioned myself on technicolor battlefields leading Marines to victory. I sought to draw some kind of parallel between the weapons of the koryu that I longed to learn and the M16 rifle and Ka-Bar fighting knife that constitute the tools of my daily trade.

Now—some twenty years later—I have been in harm's way using those tools and have trained in the koryu, and the parallel is clear. There is no magic secret or dramatic fields of glory. There is hard work, commitment, focused application, and a fusion of the mental and physical that creates an ethos—the ethos of the warrior.

Within these pages, Diane Skoss—herself a dedicated exponent of the koryu bujutsu—has brought together the thoughts, musings, and expertise of a group of today's foremost practitioners of this time-honored but heretofore little-chronicled calling. I am asked by many why—after many years of judo, jujutsu, and other military systems of close combat—I chose to "start over," turn in my "black belts" and begin this journey. My answer is simple: of all the forms of training I have encountered, the koryu bujutsu provide mind and body applications that are the closest to actual combat.

I am confident that any reader will find much within this volume to challenge his or her preconceived notions. And while Diane has clearly taken a quantum leap with this effort, I hope that she will allow me to close by saying that a book is only the first step. For those intrigued by these pages, find a koryu teacher, grasp a weapon, and train. You will feel something altogether different when the tip of a *jo* lies two inches from the bridge of your nose or a *yari* thrust that you initiate is parried and your opponent's thrust hits home. And when you do, you will find that concerns about weapon type, uniform patches, and your gradings in other martial arts fade away.

Instead, you will be left to deal with the feeling that each warrior who has gone into combat has faced: am I good enough today, this minute, right now? And if you find yourself lacking—and many times this will be the case—you will train harder, looking for answers not in a better weapon or a mystic adage, but within the inner reaches of yourself. For in the core of combatives, it is not the weapon, it is the warrior who wields it; it is not the magic, it is the mindset.

You will walk away changed, of this I have no doubt. And change is the paradigm that makes the koryu what it is. The weapons and training methods do not change—the exponent does. In a fast-paced world of crisis and short-lived fads or flavors of the month, this point of reference is definitely needed. For conflicts will occur, and warriors will engage. In the final analysis, mindset—and the training that fosters it—will prevail.

And mindset—the combat mindset—is the heart of the koryu.

Semper Fidelis.

Major George H. Bristol
United States Marine Corps

PREFACE

The idea for this book descended upon me in a way somewhat akin to the martial revelations you'll read about in these pages. I was sitting at my mother's kitchen table, one very early morning just thirty minutes before I had to leave to catch my flight back to Japan. I was at one of those frustrating points in life—not entirely happy with my work, weary of the daily struggle of life in Japan, and in desperate need of some change. I sat there drinking my coffee and dreading my flight.

Suddenly, almost as if someone or something had whispered the words to me, I thought, "Why not publish something on the classical martial arts?" The idea was exquisite, combining book-making—my favorite part of work—with my favorite subject, the *koryu*. As soon as I got back to Tokyo I set to work. It took nearly a year and a half to set up a company, line up authors, create a marketing strategy, arrange for printing, warehousing, and mailing, but the inspiration has, at last, become reality—*Koryu Bujutsu: The Classical Warrior Traditions of Japan.*

I did not make the journey on my own. This book would not exist without my five contributors, to whom I owe the most profound thanks. Inoue Kazuhiro generously provided me with a number of splendid photographs, featured on the cover and in the "Field Guide." Marci Bird did a brilliant job translating Meik's interview with Sawada Sensei, and Derek Steel not only provided the translation of Liam's interview with Kato Sensei, but also acted as "the editor's editor," forcing me back to the drawing board mercilessly as I wrestled with the introduction.

My life partner and husband, Meik, wrote for me, did proofreading, made coffee, washed the dishes, did laundry, and in general took good care of me while this book was in gestation. Lisa Fenster kept me sane and balanced. Karen Schmucker, Eric Montes, Richard Florence, and my parents also contributed hugely to this project.

One of the great challenges when working in a subject area that requires the use of Japanese terminology is deciding how to render those terms effectively in an English text. I drew on the advice of a number of experts[1] in preparing guidelines for the publications of Koryu Books. The results of our efforts, "The Koryu Books Japanese Style Sheet," is available to anyone interested in the details of discussions and decisions.[2] The basics: Japanese personal names are given in natural Japanese order, with the family name first. All Japanese terms are italicized on their first appearance and are for the most part defined in the text, and appear in the glossary, together with their kanji. I have decided, for the present, not to indicate Japanese long vowels in the text, but hope in future to incorporate them into at least the glossary.

Thanks are also due to the latest technologies, from my trusty no-longer-quite-new Micron Pentium tower, to my nifty Zip drive; for once (knock on wood), all the parts worked together, without major breakdowns. The Internet has also opened up new possibilities, including a monthly on-line magazine. *Koryu.com* has been designed to supplement the information in *Koryu Bujutsu,* and it can be found at http:/Koryu.com. Visit soon to read more articles by the contributors, and to view more photographs; be sure to register for our electronic mailing list.

As hard as we all have worked on this book, it is inevitable that errors have crept in, and have evaded my blurry eyes. If you find one, don't blame it on my contributors or translators, for the responsibility lies entirely with me.

Diane Skoss

---

[1]Ellis Amdur, Hunter Armstrong, Ron Beaubien, Alex Bennett, Larry Bieri, *Randy Channel, Richard Florence, Dave Hall, David Lynch, Dave Lowry, Wayne Muromoto, David Pitard, Guy Power, Stanley Pranin, Meik Skoss, Derek Steel, and Mark Wiley.

[2]The current version is at the Koryu Books ftp site: ftp.koryubooks.com; the file is called stylesheet.txt.

Diane Skoss initially went to Japan in 1987 to further her study of aikido. Her path has led in some surprising (at least to her) directions, and she now trains in several classical and modern martial arts. For six years she was managing editor of Aikido Journal; *her responsibilities there also included book design and production. In 1996 she founded her own publishing company, Koryu Books. This is her first publication.*

INTRODUCTION: *Keiko Shokon*

Diane Skoss

EXPLORE THE OLD

"By exploring the old, one becomes able to understand the new."
Kato Takashi, headmaster of the Tatsumi-ryu, draws on Confucius to
describe the value of the classical martial arts in today's society. In a
similar vein, my own teacher's teacher, Nishioka Tsuneo, has as his
motto, *"Keiko shokon:* Reflect deeply on the past, decide what to do
now, then do it," urging us to connect our studies of ancient arts with
decisive action in our daily lives. The stream of the *koryu bujutsu,* or
classical martial traditions, flows down to us across more than four centuries, and provides a unique vehicle for both reflecting on the past and
actualizing the present.

Training in the classical martial arts takes place within the context of
a time-honored and very Japanese social structure that has at its center
the transmission of tradition. These arts can be thought of as living history, preserving principles of combat and details of etiquette of an era
long past. Yet they also serve a multitude of purposes in our modern
world, ranging from "spiritual forging" to the cultivation of skills that
are practical despite the archaic weapons employed. It comes as no surprise, then, that growing numbers of Westerners are becoming interested in these ancient Japanese arts.

The problem is that the secrets of these traditions are not revealed
casually or quickly, and nearly all of those who are able to truly trans-
mit *koryu* (classical) techniques and teachings are located in Japan.
Isshin denshin, a direct communication that occurs almost "telepathi-
cally" from the spirit of the teacher to that of the student is the only
way to partake of the continuing transmission of a classical tradition. A
decade, or three, is required; for many people in the West this just isn't
practical. Still, while it may be difficult to actually wet your feet, let
alone become immersed, in the stream of the koryu, there *are* other

ways to benefit from some of the insights to be found in these classical arts.

Watching demonstrations of the koryu, talking with and listening to experienced practitioners and instructors, and reading and reflecting on the histories and lessons handed down from the past are a few of the more readily accessible approaches. One of the best places to begin is with the work of the late Donn F. Draeger, who was the first to write in any detail about the history of Japanese martial arts. He provided definitions and descriptions that after twenty-five years are still the most reliable starting point for any inquiry into the koryu bujutsu. I hope this volume will be a natural second step.

My goal has been to assemble a collection of essays by writers with impeccable credentials, not only as researchers, but as thinkers and educators, and, most importantly, as practitioners of the Japanese classical martial traditions. The five contributors to this volume have spent long years in Japan, training and getting to know the people who know the most about the classical arts. They are all licensed in one or more authentic classical traditions. They have direct and personal contact with headmasters and head instructors of many ryu in addition to their own—with them they have trained, wandered among castle ruins, researched lineages, explored musty bookshops, pored over fragile scrolls, visited ancient battlefields, gone shopping for blades, deciphered old-style writings, paid their respects at shrines, discussed relative merits of weapons and techniques, attended funerals, argued historical details, and drank in celebration. These experiences and connections, together with the fact that they are all native speakers of English, put them in a rather unique position to discuss the subtleties of the koryu bujutsu.

MEET THE CONTRIBUTORS

I met the first of these exceptional men in 1988, about a year and a half after my arrival in Japan, while researching an article on *naginata.* I had discovered that a small group was doing some sort of "old-style" naginata in the Waseda University aikido dojo just before my regular Saturday aikido practice. Someone mentioned to me that one of the members of this naginata school was a "a foreign guy, who seemed to know a lot about martial arts," so I arrived for practice early one day to watch.

Meik Skoss, a.k.a. the "knowledgeable foreigner," proved to be just that. He sat at the edge of the dojo looking the epitome of the immutable Japanese martial arts instructor, despite his American face. He answered my questions politely, explaining that the lower postures and bent knees of Toda-ha Buko-ryu were due to both the greater weight of the weapon and the fact that the techniques were designed to be done while wearing armor. He then proceeded to regale me with what turned into two pages of densely written notes on the history and techniques of the school.

Nearly ten years later, I am no longer in awe of this formidable researcher, instructor, and student of the classical martial arts. In fact, through some odd twist of fate, we are now married! (Those of you who are interested can read more of *that* story in Wayne Muromoto's profile in *Furyu: The Budo Journal* 1, no. 4:33-34).

I first encountered Liam Keeley at a Japan Martial Arts Society meeting in March, 1989. JMAS was established in 1983 for non-Japanese interested in the study of modern and traditional martial arts. This organization was founded by some of the most senior foreign practitioners in Japan, including Chairman Phil Relnick, who first came to Japan in the mid-1950s. Through quarterly demonstrations and an accompanying newsletter, JMAS provided a valuable network for non-Japanese martial artists in Japan, until 1991, when it quietly fell dormant.

The March meeting focused on "Judo in Japan and Abroad" and featured Osawa Yoshimi and members of the Waseda University Judo Club. Afterwards, we gathered at the local Victoria Station (a more-or-less Western-style restaurant), where I got the chance to become acquainted with Liam.

An ex-South African, now an Irish citizen, he is the only person I know who has practiced an African fighting art, one of the very few outsiders to ever learn Zulu stick-fighting. He was also one of Draeger's team, along with Meik Skoss and Hunter Armstrong, on his hoplological field studies in Indonesia. Liam impresses with his solid imperturbability, both on the dojo floor and in his "real" life, as husband and father of three. It was quite a surprise to discover just recently that he had not always had such a reputation—during his Goju-ryu karate days at Higaonna Sensei's Yoyogi dojo, he had, in fact, been considered quite a hot-head! In short, he is a formidable example of the effects of diligent and correct training.

It was at another JMAS meeting that I met Dave Hall, who was then hard at work on his Ph.D. dissertation, *Marishiten: Buddhism and the Warrior Goddess*, from which his contribution to this book is derived. We used to run into each other quite often at the Wendy's in Shinjuku. This is not as odd as it sounds, as that particular Wendy's was just across the street from the largest English language bookstore in town. More importantly, at that time decent salad bars were a rarity anywhere in Tokyo, and Wendy's was the only fast-food restaurant (i.e. one that you could possibly afford) that offered such fare. Best of all, at least according to Dave, was the fact that during the summer months the salad bar included watermelon, another expensive rarity in Japan. He developed a technique for stacking a large quantity of watermelon chunks on a single salad bar plate. He'd then retire to a table in back to feast and work on his dissertation. And that is where I would often find him when I stopped in after my book-buying expeditions.

We had many a lively discussion about martial arts and editing, since he had been involved with the *JMAS Newsletter* and I had just taken a position as editor for what was then *Aiki News*. Dave was the first to point out to me the fact that Zen was not necessarily the only, or even the most important, religious influence on the Japanese martial arts. Esoteric Buddhism, or *mikkyo,* played a profound role in the world of the Japanese *bushi* (warrior). In order to better understand this connection, Dave was undergoing the full course of training for ordination as a Tendai priest. In the process, he learned a number of esoteric rituals, including some related to Marishiten, the warrior goddess of his dissertation.

Dave's departure from Japan in October of 1990 curtailed our chats until several years later, when Meik and I visited him and his family in California. This time, instead of sitting comfortably across a table discussing warrior goddesses, I had the opportunity to face Dave with only a stick between me and his wooden sword. I had not been training in *jo* long, and he kindly introduced me to some of the subtle nuances of Draeger's approach to Shindo Muso-ryu,[1] which included finishing strikes in a closer proximity to one's face than I had previously encountered!

Hunter "Chip" Armstrong and I first became acquainted in 1990, at the Second International Seminar of Budo Culture. This annual event, organized by the Nippon Budokan Foundation, was created, according to its sponsors, to deepen the understanding of historical, philosophic, and scientific aspects of budo, to increase mutual friendship, and to internationalize Japanese traditional culture.

One of the more interesting features of this seminar is the "New Budo Experience" session, when participants can spend a few hours "trying out" an unfamiliar martial art. Expert instructors provide brief introductory classes in judo, kendo, kyudo, karatedo, aikido, Shorinji kempo, naginata, jukendo, and sumo. Jukendo, or bayonet fencing, was offered for the first time that year, and a group of us, including Meik, Liam, Chip, and myself, jumped at the opportunity to try this most unusual art.

Chip left soon after for the States, first to the Big Island of Hawaii, later to settle in Arizona. As Draeger's successor to the directorship of the International Hoplology Society and co-editor of their newsletter, *Hoplos*, he maintains the extensive IHS library and is a ceaseless fount of information. He's also fond of barefoot treks, accompanied by his son Hunter, and their half-coyote dog, Tengu, up the magnificent rock buttes that fill the view from his living room window.

---

[1] The characters for this school's name, 神道, may be transcribed or pronounced either "Shindo," or "Shinto." My own teacher prefers "Shinto," and this is the form I generally use. However, a number of my seniors, not to mention Draeger himself, consistently use/d "Shindo," so I use this form when writing of them and their training. The two terms are identical.

Ellis Amdur left Japan about the time I arrived, so for many years he was to me just a figure in photos, an author of articles in back issues of the *JMAS Newsletter*, and a voice on a videotape. I finally met him in the flesh during a brief visit to Seattle in 1992. We spent our two days visiting dojos, training, and chatting, in the course of which he mentioned that he'd been doing some writing about *aiki*. As an editor, I was always on the lookout for intelligently written, thoughtful material, and my interest was piqued.

Sure enough, his first submission challenged many of the aikido world's treasured notions, and as a contributing editor to *Aikido Journal,* he has gone on to write profound, sometimes disturbing, reflections on aikido training today. Working with his series of insightful and provocative "Improvisations" was one of the highlights of producing each issue.

Ellis now trains and teaches in Seattle, where he is raising two bright, athletic sons. Wisely, he has encouraged them to take up the Brazilian martial art of *capoeira* (in addition to their number one passion, soccer), which he himself has never practiced. Special dojo occasions now include a performance by capoeristas, the chants, music, and exuberance a striking contrast to the formality of the classical Japanese traditions.

Shades of Gray

The expertise of these contributors is everywhere apparent in the chapters that follow and the effect is cumulative. Themes echo, reverberate, and connect in illuminating configurations, and the threads running throughout the book are well worth puzzling out. I won't explicate further here, except to point out what I believe to be one of the most important lessons revealed in these pages: variation and differences are the only certainty when speaking of the koryu bujutsu. You'll find vastly different, yet equally valid definitions, explanations of purpose, and even terminology. As one of my teachers, Phil Relnick, is fond of saying, there is no black or white. In koryu, as in Japan in general, black and white can often both be true simultaneously, giving rise to a rich variety of grays. Recognizing that there is no need for "either/or" and that more than one seemingly contradictory thing can be true at the same time is one of the most difficult, yet essential, concepts for the Westerner interested in these arts to internalize. Perhaps these writers and their essays can make that understanding just one shade easier.

Hunter B. Armstrong has been training in the classical martial arts for more than twenty years, and he currently practices Shindo Muso-ryu jojutsu, Shinkage-ryu heiho, and Owari Kan-ryu sojutsu. As Director of the International Hoplology Society, he has continued the research and data collection efforts begun by IHS founder Donn F. Draeger.

THE KORYU BUJUTSU EXPERIENCE

Hunter B. Armstrong

From the hoplological[1] perspective, Japan's *koryu bujutsu* are among the last extant hand-to-hand battlefield martial fighting arts in the world. As such, they provide a unique window on the history of Japan's martial culture, and a glimpse into an aspect of human behavior rarely seen in today's high-tech, materialistic world. They are training not only in movements necessary for survival on a medieval battlefield, but for human interaction and behavior that had to rise above the pettiness of personal squabbles to a level of morality and ethics that today is grossly misunderstood.

KORYU BUJUTSU DEFINED

First, I should define what I mean by koryu bujutsu training. *Koryu* is made up of two characters: 古 *ko* or *furu(i)*, meaning "old," and 流 *ryu* or *naga(reru)*, meaning "flow." The latter, in combination with other characters, is often used to refer to styles, schools, or traditions of behavior, movement, or thought. In Japan, names of styles or schools of flower arrangement, dance, tea ceremony, calligraphy, and fighting arts, among others, have the suffix "-*ryu*" appended. Thus, koryu specifically refers to "old styles, schools, or traditions." I prefer "old traditions."

Here, we are specifically concerned with old traditions of Japanese martial arts. "Martial arts" is denoted by the second word, *bujutsu* (as

---

[1] Hoplology is the study of human combative behavior and performance.

opposed to *budo*—martial ways). It should be noted, however, that koryu bujutsu does not include Okinawan fighting arts. This is not because the Okinawan arts are not worthy, but because they have their own distinct cultural background and legacy, and deserve better than to be lumped in as poor cousins of the Japanese fighting arts.[2]

The next question then, is how to define the "old" in koryu. This is not easily done; in fact it is arbitrary and frequently based upon opinion. However, in my opinion, old refers primarily to time of origin. Thus, the koryu are those traditions that originated sometime up to and including the early Tokugawa period (1603-1868). However, the caveat here is that we Westerners often try to discriminate too finely. Life, and certainly cultural evolution, is rarely clean-cut and distinct. We have to look at other aspects beyond the time frame when defining koryu bujutsu.

The second major factor is structural integrity, in other words, how well has the tradition been maintained or how much of it has been reconstructed. Retaining the original structure of the tradition (the ryu) and its bujutsu—the techniques and their applications—was/is based on how the members of the ryu have maintained and continue to maintain its original functional aims and practice. In this regard, Donn Draeger elucidated an interesting and valid distinction between the functional priorities of classical bujutsu and budo. For the more modern arts of budo, the ranking of priorities is (1) morals, (2) discipline, (3) aesthetic form. For the older bujutsu, in contrast, the emphasis was on (1) combat, (2) discipline, (3) morals (Draeger 1973, 36).

The koryu bujutsu can then be defined as "traditions of fighting arts originating no later than the early Tokugawa period, and whose functional aims were the development of combat effectiveness, discipline, and morality, in that order." Of course, there are exceptions and varia-

---

[2] It should also be noted that, strictly speaking, the fighting arts of Okinawa were not part of traditions or ryu, in the Japanese sense. Thus, the term "koryu bujutsu" is meaningless when applied to Okinawa.

tions, but this definition can serve as a rough outline on which to base this discussion.

WEAPONS AND HEIHO

On the battlefield the *bushi* (warrior) was likely to encounter a number of different weapons, including various types of *yari* (spear), *naginata* (Japanese glaive), *nagamaki* (another sort of Japanese glaive), *yumi* (bow), not to mention the Japanese sword in its various configurations. If the warrior was to survive against these weapons, and more importantly, dominate, it was imperative that he be skilled in their use. Due to the demands of battlefield reality, most if not all of the early koryu were *sogo bujutsu* (integrated, composite martial arts/systems).

Designed for the battlefield, the classical arts incorporated training in a variety of weapons systems, including grappling with weapons and in armor.[3] Unlike modern styles, such as kendo, judo, aikido (yes, *aikijutsu* too), *atarashii naginata*, etc., that are derived from *kobujutsu* ("old" bujutsu), the classical traditions did not specialize in one weapon or type of combat. The use of the various weapons and martial systems were interrelated and integrated through a core set of principles, *heiho*.[4] This heiho was, and is still, handed down from the founder through each headmaster. In their heiho, the classical traditions placed their technical emphasis on the use of weaponry, with the sword at the center. The use of those weapons was and is distinctly different in intent and function from the weapon arts of modern budo. And by extension, the classical systems' body arts—*kogusoku, yawara, jujutsu, kumiuchi,* etc.—also have different ends and functions than their more modern descendants.

---

[3] Actual empty-hand training was far down on the priority list of battlefield needs. Indeed, much of what we now call "empty-hand" training was actually some variation of grappling with weapons.

[4] Heiho is often defined as "military tactics." Perhaps a more appropriate interpretation would be "martial principles."

KATA

The bujutsu training methods were designed for developing the potential of the individual bushi to not only survive, but to dominate on the battlefield. In Japan, a socio-cultural milieu developed in which the warrior-combatant was at the top or near the top of society for several hundred years. While there have been warrior aristocrats in other cultures, few have lasted at the top of their societies for as long as the bushi maintained his status in Japan. This position allowed for the development and refinement of a martial culture of a depth and scope that was probably unparalleled in any other country.

In this warrior-based context, principles were elucidated and put into practice that are only now being recognized for their sophistication in understanding of human behavior in combat and elegance in enhancing that behavior.[5] Not so surprisingly, the primary elements of training are similar in the bujutsu of all the koryu. The foundation for all is the practice of partnered prearranged movement/behavior patterns, or two-man *kata*. For it is within the context of the kata that the teacher can teach all aspects of combat, from basic movement, to complexes of movement-and-behavior.

Kata as generally performed today in the modern budo have been adapted to new contexts. Many of the modern budo have instituted divisions in their training. Typically, kendo, judo, karatedo, atarashii naginata, and *jukendo* (way of the bayonet), for example, divide their training between prearranged movement training and free exchanges. In judo, the divisions are kata and *randori*; in kendo, atarashii naginata and jukendo, they are kata and *jigeiko;* and in karatedo, they are kata and *kumite.* Generally speaking, the free exchange tends to be considered a better combative training, while the kata is thought of as a more

---

[5] For example, Yagyu Nobuharu, headmaster of the Owari line of Yagyu Shinkage-ryu, and his students gave a demonstration of kata as training for complex decision-making at the "Breakthroughs in Knowledge Toward the 21st Century—People, Technology, & Society: '96 Japan-Germany Symposium on 'Place and Syntopy,'" held on December 3, 1996 at the German Culture Center in Tokyo.

aesthetic and spiritual training medium. In many of the modern budo, kata is seen to have little or no combative application.

In contrast, the kata of the koryu bujutsu was the core of all training. The only "free exchange" training was either a real fight or a test of what one had learned in the kata. Again, it must be understood that kata was more than merely training basic movements. I addressed this in a several different issues of *Hoplos*, the journal of the International Hoplology Society:

> The kata were profound systems of integrated movements and *behaviors*. The purpose of kata (or any prearranged movement pattern) designed for combative application was not to develop the individual's ability to respond to any attack with the choice of a wide variety of techniques, but to train that individual to *effectively utilize a select few proven techniques in response to a wide variety of attacks or combative situations*. To this end, a particular system or style might contain a large number of prearranged movement patterns, composed of those techniques that had been proven survival efficient in actual combat.
>
> The original kata (and their applications) were developed from combative experience, and evolved through roughly three hundred years of combative activity. The kata were not analyzed and then practiced; on the contrary, it was personal combat that was analyzed, and elements were extracted that could be simulated and practiced... as kata. Once the combat experience was no longer the primary base for the development or evolution of the technique, and the techniques become innovations of individuals based on their analysis of kata rather than their personal combative experience, then we begin to see changes in the patterns, and a shift in emphasis from simulating combat, to other aims, leading to a change even in the basic techniques. (Armstrong 1988, 20)

In weapons-/fighting systems designed for mortal combat—as the koryu bujutsu were—the inherent dangers in training with lethal weapons aimed at potentially fatal targets precludes the use of a free-sparring type action. In some cases this danger has been avoided through the development of protective armor. However, training armor itself is a limiting factor and imposes changes upon the patterns of movement (angles and targeting), and more importantly, the psychological components of combat—the feeling of safety while training cannot prepare the individual for the psychological stress from the danger/threat inherent in mortal combat. Preparation to withstand such stress can only be readily approached in training through the use of actual weapons (or potentially dangerous simulated or rebated weapons), utilizing prearranged patterns of movement in which the potential for danger arises from any errors made in timing or movement; these errors can then be utilized by either opponent by momentarily breaking the prearranged pattern, and attacking the opening *(suki)* that is created. Such a system of training forces the practitioner to attempt to perfect both his ability to perform the patterned movements (timing, distancing, targeting, etc.) and, as important, to develop his ability to take spontaneous advantage of his opponent's errors or to cover his own; the lack of such ability incurs pain at the least, and severe injury or death in the extreme. Thus, the system for preparing the participant (combatant) for mortal combat provides a context in which concentration on the psychological aspects (behavior and attitudes) is approached at least as strongly as are movement patterns. Ergo, the psycho-physical content of the movement/behavior patterns seen in most mortal combative systems is perhaps the major distinguishing feature. (Armstrong 1991, 28)

Koryu bujutsu training is kata. Today, it is a unique method of training that is only superficially similar to the kata of modern budo. The aim of the classical training was and is not simply the learning of movement techniques, but the development of combative behaviors that prepare one for implementing simple-but-learned-movement techniques in the face of the overwhelmingly traumatic stress of combat. No amount of solo training or simple movement training will do that. However, even empty-hand training *with an opponent with combative intent* has been shown to be effective for non-empty-hand combat. It is the behavioral aspect that is most important, not the simple movement patterns. But, the behavioral aspects can only be trained through movement patterns learned and practiced with opponents. This is why all combatively functional training systems in all cultures put their emphasis on training with an opponent in as realistic as possible a manner, and that is in prearranged patterns as versus free-exchanges that have been cushioned for safety.

KORYU—A LIVING ENTITY

Perhaps one of the most important distinctions between modern budo and koryu bujutsu is the organizational structure of the entity encompassing the arts. A true koryu is a living entity, one that subsumes the individual. For the individual, it is a relationship with a living legacy and with the people within that heritage, living, dead, and yet to be born. This relationship is difficult to comprehend for those who are not members of a koryu, and especially so for those who have not spent time in Japan. The connections within the ryu's social nexus and between the ryu and its ancestral shrines in Japan are of great importance to the ryu.

In the classical tradition that maintains its traditional practices (as opposed to a reconstructed one), there is generally one *dojo* under the guidance of the *sensei*. There are no "branch dojo" under junior instructors.[6] The hierarchy is a simple one: the one sensei and the students. While

---

[6] Of course, there are cases where a ryu member has *menkyo* (license) and is teaching at his own dojo. However, in such situations, the students of the menkyo holder are not ipso facto students of the headmaster; though they might be members of the ryu, in most cases they are students strictly of their teacher.

those who are more junior show respect to their seniors, those who are more senior show an equal, if different, kind of respect to their juniors. There is no sharp line of demarcation between one level and another. It is not a hierarchy of social standing, but merely an acknowledgment of experience and knowledge. It bears no relationship to the sharp distinction between *sempai* (senior) and *kohai* (junior) that is often found in the modern budo dojo. There is no ranking system per se to distinguish members in social situations as there are in many of the modern budo, especially those associated with Japan's education system. There are no *mudansha* (in the modern budo, literally, "non-graded," or below black belt level) who are expected to follow the directions and commands of *yudansha* (those holding black belt rank). There are only the sensei's students.

BUDO FOR THE MASSES; BUJUTSU FOR INDIVIDUALS

Here, some explanation regarding the senior-junior relationship and related etiquette often seen in the modern budo dojo, especially those connected to the Japanese education system, may be necessary. In the thirty-year period leading up to World War II, Japan's education system was increasingly influenced by the Japanese military.[7] By the time of the war, martial arts training in the schools had become an integral part of the program for inculcating militaristic and nationalist fervor in the populace. Much of the institutionalized budo training took on a military flavor, including military-type distinctions in rank and position. This was accompanied by much of the etiquette and posturing used by the military—standing in lines at attention, hands rigidly held at the pant-seam line; seniors barking orders at juniors; juniors barking "*Ossu*" in response to seniors; large groups of students practicing standardized patterns in synchrony. Not only did much of this have little to do with traditional Japanese training, it had even less to do with train-

---

[7] For some interesting background on this influence see *The Development of the Combative Arts and Ways within Japan's Modern Education System* (Hargrave 1996).

ing the individual for combat. Its aim was to develop a strong and cohesive group mentality, instilled with militant, nationalistic fervor. This behavior was strictly the result of the military's influence on budo training in the schools, and did not stem from the influence of traditional bushi behavior. Interestingly, this militaristic behavior continues today in the education system of modern, "pacifist" Japan.

Today, modern budo organizations make little, if any, attempt to maintain koryu structure and integrity. Karate, aikido, judo, and kendo, are all organized following essentially a single pattern. The kata and techniques have been standardized (with periodic updating), and *dan* rankings established that are generally paralleled by a level of kata. These rankings are typically awarded according to an individual's standing in the organization, and are based on seniority, testing, and sometimes, competition. At a certain, relatively high, dan level, the test for rank is conducted by a board of senior members of the organization. All this is at least partially a result of the previously described prewar influences on the budo by the government, military, and education systems.

While the aim now in the modern budo organizations is not enhanced nationalistic feeling, they do have as a goal group identity and cohesion, rather than individual functional proficiency. Such technical standardization emphasizes group sameness, but may not be too concerned with enhancing individual capability. On the other hand, these standardized movements allow for training large numbers of people at the same time, a necessity for the large modern budo organizations, which often actively seek new members and work to spread into new areas.

In contrast, the koryu that maintain their old ways utilize a training structure that is aimed at attaining the individual's potential. Intensive in both time and energy, this type of training is not conducive to large group instruction. In essence, the classical koryu must maintain a quality standard that precludes quantity. In addition, the maintenance of the integrity of the koryu demands a dedication from its members that is found only in a few people who are willing to go to the considerable time, trouble, and expense that membership entails. So, while the modern budo organizations look to numbers and expansion to achieve their goals, the koryu look to quality and consolidation. Unfortunately, the structure of the koryu is not as well-suited to today's world as that of the modern budo organizations. It is likely that the koryu will have to take on some of the characteristics of the modern organizations in order to survive, and this has already begun to happen.

Unlike the standardized, group emphasis of the modern budo, the instructional relationship in the koryu tends to be a very personal one between teacher and student. The standardization that does exist is aimed at providing a model for the beginner to follow easily; one from which he is expected eventually to break away. The sensei teaches directly to the individual abilities, traits, and potentials of the student. A member of the ryu is a personal student of the ryu's headmaster, not of some junior or assistant instructor at a branch dojo. There is no more standardization in true koryu training than there is standardization in individuals. Because of that one-to-one relationship, the sensei is a mentor in the maturing of the *deshi* (disciple or student). He is the conduit through which the techniques, values, and traditions are passed on to each generation. This is the way the teacher teaches; it was the way he was taught. It is part of the "revelation" that has been passed on from one inheritor to the next. Obviously, not everyone who trains in the koryu can become a teacher, and few receive full teaching *menkyo* (license or certification). For those who do, it is because they have demonstrated an ability to understand not only the essence of the tradition, but an ability to teach the essence in a manner that matches the capabilities of each individual student.

This process of revelation from teacher to student is the basis of koryu bujutsu. To achieve a useful level of understanding and physical skill, it was absolutely necessary for partner training to be conducted by the teacher in a manner that was stressful and filled not only with a simulation of danger, but with the actual danger of severe injury and the potential for death. Modern sports science and sports psychology tells us that we can use the training hall for learning new skills and refining them, and to a certain extent, the training hall can prepare us for the psychological stress of competition. But the training hall can do little to prepare us for facing an enemy who seeks to do us harm or to kill us. While the learning and practicing of techniques (skills) in the dojo can prepare us for the physical action, the only way to prepare for the use of combative techniques in the stress of combat is to face that stress while training. This was well understood in the classical dojo, but it seems often to have been forgotten in modern budo.

In the koryu bujutsu dojo, the only person with the competence to apply such danger in a learning situation and tune it to the capability of the student, and thus to pass on the revelation, was/is the sensei. Without forging on the anvil of partner training, permeated with danger/threat, true spirituality is lost; the revelation is not renewed. The trainee must be put through the crucible of reality—the consequences of both training for and engaging in *real* combat—in order to be psychologically prepared for the rigors of real combat. That is what the martial spiritual revelation is all about.

While *shugyo* (austere training) takes place in a "spiritual location"—a dojo (place of the path)—the training does not include philosophical, spiritual discourse on the meaning of the revelation. It consists of facing danger and one's own fear while executing effective combative technique. The trainees of any particular ryu who reach a full spiritual understanding are very few. Even in modern times, it is for this older meaning of spirit that the koryu is preparing the student... if he has the potential.

"Spiritual" Koryu Bujutsu

Today, there are many Japanese koryu teachers who still believe that the ideal moral and spiritual qualities—honor, integrity, responsibility-and-obligation, to name a few—as intuitively taught in the koryu are as valid today as they were in the heyday of the bushi. Certainly the ideals were not achieved by all, but they were and are present as goals toward which to strive.

If one considers that the koryu evolved to train warriors to survive not only the rigors of the battlefield, but the life-and-death nature of the bushi lifestyle as well, then it is possible to understand the importance of the individual relationship within the koryu, and the emphasis on teaching to each student's capabilities—mental, physical, and spiritual. However, this is not the spirituality we often hear spoken of in the modern dojo. Many modern spiritually-oriented people in budo are more than willing to expound on the "spiritual benefits" of training. Books on Zen are cited, and such esoterica as "the acceptance of death" are discussed. However, much less politically correct is the demand of the koryu that one not only accept one's own death, but also that one must develop the will to kill another. It is easy to die; it is not so easy to consciously, willingly, take the life of another. It was for this that the koryu was preparing the classical warrior—to face death... his own and another's. Only by having the capability to kill can one truly show the compassion of not killing. As one wag put it recently, you can show mercy only if you are the winner. You can only truly understand life if you accept death as part of it. This is the "spiritual" part of koryu bujutsu.

Yet, in a koryu dojo in Japan, you will hardly ever hear anyone mention anything to do with spiritual matters. You're far more likely to hear stories about bushi of old. The spirituality of the traditions is tied to the shrines and sites where the founders are said to have received their martial revelations. Those revelations have "flowed down" (流 nagareru/ryu) via the chain of headmasters. They are transmitted in the teachings and techniques—as they are doled out by the sensei—and internalized and renewed under his direct tutelage over a period of years—and through arduous training with fellow members of the tradition. The "spiritual" aspect of the koryu has little to do with that of modern budo.

Some talk of the morality inculcated through training, for example, in *iaido*. Somehow, by working alone with "the sword and the mind" (to coin a phrase), one is supposed to rise above the common, immoral world. The question is, as morality refers to people interacting, how can it be learned in a solo training context? If any moral improvement is to occur, then it must be in a social context, between interacting individuals. *Battojutsu*, iaido's classical antecedent, is part of a larger training matrix of *koryu kenjutsu*. Here, there is a context for the give-and-take between opponents; here is the basis for "making a better person." And, while the ultimate barrier likely is one's own mind, it is so in the context of fear and stress in combat with another. The only way to train the mind to deal with that stress is to train it in a context that simulates the reality that produces that stress. In their pure form, the koryu bujutsu are not fun, they are not "spiritual" or "moral" in the way that term is used in the modern budo. As David Hall, Ph.D., pithily put it, "The morality of the classical warrior fits better with the SAS or SEALS than with Tohei aikido."

BATTO AND IAIDO

By looking at those classical traditions that have maintained their structural integrity to some degree, we can clearly see the differences between the classical and modern combative systems. The koryu arts of *iaijutsu* or battojutsu (sword-drawing), kenjutsu (swordsmanship), *naginatajutsu* (glaive arts), *sojutsu* (spearmanship), kogusoku (armored grappling), etc., differ from their modern derivations (iaido, kendo, atarashii naginata, judo, aikido, etc.) in both form and content. The koryu systems have even less connection with the more recent developments in budo, such as jukendo, *tankendo* (short sword way), and karatedo.

To better illustrate some of these differences, we can compare iaido with the apparently similar koryu art of *batto* (iaijutsu).[8] While iaido and koryu batto have very obvious similarities, there are equally vast differences. Iaido,[9] by definition, is the solo practice of drawing the Japanese sword. This is generally done independently of other sword

---

[8] Although some ryu might have more specific usage of these two terms, they are often considered synonymous. For simplicity's sake, I'll use the term "batto." A distinction should be made between koryu batto and several modern sword-drawing arts that use these terms in their names. Toyama-ryu *battodo*, for example, is a modern sword-drawing, test-cutting system. While quite effective at what it was designed for, i.e., sword-drawing and test-cutting, it has little or no battlefield application.

[9] The word *iai* (居合) has the connotation of "being present; in place." *Iainuki* is generally translated as "quick sword display," but literally might be viewed as "draw in place" (see fn. 10, below).

arts, although it is often organizationally linked to modern kendo. Classical batto, on the other hand, is not an independent skill. Generally, batto that is practiced as part of a classical ryu is closely integrated with the practice of the tradition's kenjutsu. Often, batto[10] is simply the solo, live-blade, practice of the ryu's kenjutsu techniques (or portions and variations thereof). The primary difference between batto and kenjutsu, then, is that the sword techniques in batto are preceded by drawing the live sword (*shinken*) from the *saya* (scabbard) rather than starting with an already drawn *bokuto* (wooden sword).[11] Then, rather than practicing the ensuing movements against an opponent as in kenjutsu, the movements are practiced solo. In essence, batto is, in this sense, simply practicing kenjutsu alone with a live blade.

Many of the more modern techniques of iaido emphasize the speed of draw and the speed of *returning* the blade to the saya, as well as the aesthetics of the movement.[12] In classical batto, these aspects are generally not of major concern. For the classical bushi (especially during the more combative periods), the only training of functional value was the training that most closely simulated reality (occasionally resulting, by the way, in serious training injuries). Only by training in this manner could the bushi be realistically prepared for combat. Solo sword-drawing practice was even less likely to prepare the bushi for combat than solo tackling practice would help an NFL tackle prepare for a game. On the battlefield, the warrior would have his weapon readied for combat long before an opponent was close enough to strike. The speed of

---

[10] Batto 抜刀, "drawing sword." The first character, 抜, "*batsu*" is also read "*nuku*," "draw." Iaijutsu and batto, or battojutsu, are often used interchangeably.

[11] It is a mistake to think of the bokuto (also *bokken*) as merely a "training" weapon. It was often used in real fighting, and was considered a formidable weapon in itself.

[12] More often than not, iaido is practiced with an *iaito*, a non-cutting-edged "sword" designed specifically for iaido practice. Such a blade obviates the need for controlled precision in cutting.

the draw was not a major factor in these situations, and certainly speedily returning the blade to its saya had little to do with combat.

In training for combat effectiveness, the factors that can be most usefully enhanced through systematic training/practice[13] are distancing, timing, targeting, and their related components. Distancing refers not only to gauging and moderating the distance between one's self and one's enemy,[14] but also to judging and contending with the reach of the opponent's weapon and its relationship to the reach of one's own weapon. On first consideration, wielding a sword might seem to use a standard distancing factor. However, wielding a sword against another sword requires a different distancing factor than wielding it against a naginata or a yari, and vice versa. Solo sword practice provides no means for learning to adjust to the demands of the enemy's weapons.

Timing is a complex of time-related judgment and body actions that is closely connected with distancing. It is a dynamic activity that requires the use of body and mind integrated in action and reaction to the stimulus of an opposing body-and-mind. Solo practice is of benefit in the development of elementary physical coordination, but is of little value in preparing to face an enemy moving through time and space, and who possesses deadly intent.

Targeting, on one level, might be thought of as simply aiming and accurately striking a selected body part. However, it is only simple when striking at a non-moving target. Against an opponent who is not only moving, but is striking back, targeting becomes a much more complex task, interwoven with distancing and timing. All three factors

[13] There is a subtle difference between training and practice: training has the nuance of *learning* in or about the performance of a skill action, while practice implies the refining through repetition of something already learned.

[14] I use "enemy" instead of "opponent" to follow the custom of many koryu, which similarly use the word *teki* (enemy) as versus *aite* (opponent). I believe this is an important and illuminating distinction between the koryu bujutsu and modern budo.

are further complicated by the stress stimulus of an enemy trying to cut you down.

When viewed from the combative perspective, it can plainly be seen that these three integrated factors can only be addressed through partner training. As solo practice—with weapon or empty-handed—provides no means of training the most important skill factors for combat, it was/is an entirely secondary means of practice for combative ends.

Batto (and other solo weapons practice) was primarily used for self-practice when one didn't have a partner. In most classical dojo, very little time was devoted to solo practice. In some modern dojo, the emphasis may have changed, but in most classical traditions in Japan, such practice is still a relatively minor part of the overall training regimen of the ryu. For example, in Shinkage-ryu (founded by Kamiizumi Ise-no-Kami) and Yagyu Shinkage-ryu (founded by Kamiizumi's student Yagyu Munetoshi), there is either no batto, or it is done as a minor part of the overall kenjutsu training. (In the Yagyukai of Yagyu Nobuharu Sensei, there is no Yagyu-ryu sword-drawing per se; however, Nobuharu's grandfather developed Yagyu Seigo-ryu batto explicitly for modern purposes.) In Shinkage-ryu, the batto is essentially a preparation for two-man, sword-drawing kenjutsu with shinken (closer still to combative reality).

The distinguishing key, again, is *realistic preparation for combat.* Iaido, whether derived from a koryu or not,[15] has no such aspiration. Its aim is the development of aesthetic sword movement and spiritual, moral training, and the emphasis varies according to the interpretation of the individual performing the art. These are fine aims, perhaps even better than seeking combative effectiveness. Why confuse the two very different ends? Yet, there are practitioners of iaido who consistently contend that their art is combatively effective and cite apocryphal rationales

---

[15] A common mistake is to assume that if a "style" of iaido has a ryu name or ryu lineage, that it then is a koryu. Iaido is *gendai budo* (modern budo) no matter what its derivation.

KORYU BUJUTSU

as proof. One that is commonly heard is that iaido was developed on the battlefield for when a warrior's spear or other weapon was broken or became useless for some reason, and he had to quickly draw his sword to defend himself and continue fighting. First of all, extremely few of the koryu practice any kind of sword-draw while wearing armor, much less quick-draw techniques. On the other hand, several of the extant koryu do practice various weapon-systems in armor, including kenjutsu, sojutsu, kogusoku, etc.[16]

If being able to perform a quick draw while wearing *katchu* (armor) was so important, one would think that the skill would have been maintained and be more evident. Secondly, and most importantly, drawing a sword while in armor is quite a different matter from drawing while wearing everyday clothes.

The bushi in armor would only draw his *tachi*[17] if he had the time and distance to effectively do so; if a fast draw was necessary, it was probably already too late for the longer blade, and he would resort to shorter weapons and grappling. When an enemy was so close or moving in so rapidly that a warrior's weapon became useless, the bushi was trained to resort to armored grappling (kumiuchi or kogusoku) with a short-bladed weapon such as a *wakizashi, yoroidoshi,* or *hachiwari.*[18] This was more effective than trying to draw his tachi or *katana.* Takenouchi-ryu and Yagyu Shingan-ryu are two well-known traditions that put a great deal of emphasis on two-man training in these types of close-in combat with shorter blades. Shinkage-ryu also practices kogusoku with *kodachi* (short sword). In any case, even if the armored quick-draw

[16] Owari Kan-ryu occasionally practices its spear kata in armor, while Yagyu Shingan-ryu and Shinkage-ryu both train in a variety of armored weapon techniques.

[17] While the tachi is a specific type of Japanese sword, here, and commonly, the word is used to refer to swords generically.

[18] The wakizashi is essentially a short sword; yoroidoshi is a dagger-like thrusting blade for use against armor; and the hachiwari, in various shapes, was typically used as a "helmet-splitter."

The Koryu Bujutsu Experience

was feasible on the battlefield, the speed of the draw is not nearly as important as awareness, distancing, timing, and targeting, none of which are aspects of solo, sword-drawing practice.

Another rationale for the iaido quick draw is its development as "samurai self-defense." Supposedly, when the warrior was attacked while walking around minding his own business, iaido training prepared him to quickly draw his sword and defend himself. This is really not much different from the rationale for the quick-draw on the battlefield. Realistically, old world or modern, if an attack occurs so quickly as to require a fast draw from an evidently non-alert defender, the defender loses. The most important principle in heiho for not being defeated by surprise is to *avoid being surprised.* The chances of surviving a sudden attack are very small. The best way to avoid being "sucker-punched" is not to be in a position that allows one to be sucker-punched. What is necessary for realistic combative situations—particularly in potential surprise attacks—is mental and physical preparedness.[19] The average bushi relied on skills gained in training with opponents, not on training by himself.

In reality, iaido, as a solo implement training discipline, has more in common with kyudo than with kenjutsu; both iaido and kyudo do not include the dynamism supplied by facing an opponent who possesses intent.

LEARNING KORYU BUJUTSU

Koryu bujutsu is perhaps both too broad and too deep to completely and accurately define. While I can attempt to compare one aspect of it—batto—with its modern cognate, iaido, it is an unfair comparison. As mentioned previously, traditional batto is not separate from the other bujutsu in the koryu to which it belongs. It is merely a part of the overall heiho of that tradition.

---

[19] Some traditions call this aware preparedness *zanshin.*

Practicing koryu bujutsu is extremely dangerous, demanding (physically and mentally), and frustrating. And it does not end after leaving the dojo. The behaviors and attitudes one develops in the koryu dojo are not left at the door. They are maintained in one's daily life and daily relations. One doesn't get to go home after training... there are innumerable social obligations with both the in-group and society at large. One becomes enculturated through koryu bujutsu.

Anyone—Japanese or foreigner—who thinks they can "learn" a koryu any other way than by going to Japan to train and becoming immersed in koryu bujutsu and its culture is fooling themselves. Without training in koryu bujutsu one cannot know what it is, much less how it is different from modern budo.

At the same time, it should be said that the great majority of people do not need koryu. The modern budo are perfect for most people, providing both the training and social factors that are really most suitable for them. If someone truly wants koryu, it is best to let them seek it out and work for it; it will not come easily.

References

Armstrong, H.B. 1991. A Further Look at Analyzing Combative Systems. *Hoplos* 7, no. 1:24-29.

———. 1988. Prearranged Movement Patterns. *Hoplos* 6, no. 1/2:18-21.

Draeger, D.F. 1973. *Classical Budo.* The Martial Arts and Ways of Japan, 2. New York & Tokyo: Weatherhill.

Hargrave, T. 1996. "The Development of the Combative Arts and Ways within Japan's Modern Education System." Masters degree thesis, University of Hawaii.

Sawada Hanae was born in 1917 and has been training for over seventy years. She holds the hanshi certification from the All-Japan Naginata Federation, and teaches both atarashii naginata and Tendo-ryu in Tokyo. Meik Skoss has been her student in Tendo-ryu since 1976. This interview was conducted on December 9, 1996 at the Shinjuku Naginata Dojo.

The Meaning of Martial Arts Training
A Conversation with Sawada Hanae

Meik Skoss

Question: Sensei, thank you very much for taking time to talk with me. I'd like to ask you to share some of your thoughts about training in both the modern and classical martial arts. I believe that your family has been involved in the martial arts for many generations, and that your father was a kendo expert. What was his name?

Sawada Sensei: Yoshida Seiko. My grandfather was also a kendo *hanshi*.[1] Everyone in my family received this rank.

From the Butokukai?[2]
Yes. It is not a rank for a particular *ryugi* (traditional style).

What was your father's style?
Shindo Munen-ryu. My grandfather also practiced a classical style, but I am not really clear on what it was and feel a bit uneasy about saying this as a fact. But it is all written down and there is a record of all

---

[1] The highest level teaching certification.

[2] The Dai Nippon Butokukai (Greater Japan Martial Virtues Society) was founded in 1895 for the purpose of promoting the practice of martial arts and developing standardized techniques and training methods in the arts of kendo, judo, and kyudo. Prior to World War II, the issuing of teaching ranks and licenses in these arts, as well as for those of *naginata* and karatedo was largely the prerogative of this organization.

the generations in my family and their styles. My ancestors were from the Marugame domain in Shikoku.

When did you start training?

I started training in second grade in my father's *dojo.* But even though I started training so long ago, you have to keep in mind that there were days when my father wasn't there, so I didn't go to train, or days that I just sat and watched. I could get away with this because I was just a child. So you can't really say that I was training, since I was only in the second grade. On top of this, I was just a little thing and was always training with people who were bigger than me. There were many times when I couldn't hit my partner because I couldn't even reach him. I didn't train with other children. It wasn't like today, when children just train with other children and not with adults. It was a lot different then; I was always getting hit.

Did you start budo because you liked it?

Of course not. We had a dojo in our house. That's why I trained.

But you must have liked it, to continue.

It wasn't really that I liked it, but rather that I had found something that was interesting. There was never any point where the training was complete. If I had thought at any time that I had finished, I am pretty sure I would have quit. But I never reached that point. I always felt there was something more for me to learn, so I continued to train.

All through the years, there were times that I hated it and times I wanted to quit for personal reasons. There were also times when I simply was not able to train and wanted to quit. But there was always something fun about *naginata* for me. I enjoyed the give-and-take with my opponents and coming to realize what to do in different situations. That was fun, so I kept training. I could keep coming back for more because I had realized there was more to naginata than met the eye. If it were an art that was easy to grasp, then I'm sure I would never have kept at it for this long. Don't you think professional baseball players must feel the same thing about their sport? It is different for them, of

*Sawada Hanae (right) demonstrating Tendo-ryu nitto technique
with Abe Tomoko at Kashima Shrine, ca. 1980.*

course, because they receive money for playing, but still… We don't receive money, so we are doing it because we enjoy it. We do it because we have found something that captivates us. So, as you can see, the attraction of martial arts is hard to understand from the outside.

Budo is not something that can be done in a day, or a year or two. With training, there is never a point where you can stop and say this is enough. There is a deeper level. The sons of *samurai* families began training when they were just little children. They began even before they shaved their heads and donned *hakama*. The number of years they trained is not comparable to the amount people train today.

The Meaning of Martial Arts Training   41

This was just in the families of the bushi, or warriors, wasn't it?

Yes, that's right. Warriors were different. Private citizens were only that. But they, too, had to protect themselves, so they practiced various martial arts among themselves. They did this in some of the towns, or in the villages; Maniwa Nen-ryu was practiced in a village in this way.

When did you begin training at the Busen? [3]

In 1934. What we, or at least I myself, did at the Butokukai in Kyoto was to practice six or seven hours a day. And we did this every day. Even though I was practicing that much, my father told me that one year was not enough. I was made to continue for two years, then three years. Most people finished after one year of practicing in this manner, then they went out to teach. But my father made me continue until the first semester of my fourth year, when I became ill with a bad case of pleurisy. Then my father finally allowed me to stop. But he still warned me that my training was insufficient.

In my student days at the Butokukai, we practiced the naginata *kata* for a long time and then we practiced kendo. In Tendo-ryu, there is both naginata and *ken* (sword). So we had matches with both naginata and ken. Then we returned to the beginning and practiced the naginata forms again. That was the way we all learned in the old days. So all the older teachers have experience with competition; we competed with kendo teachers. We did training in the forms, then competition. Then the cycle began again.

You mentioned Tendo-ryu. I believe you studied directly under the former headmaster, Mitamura Chiyo. Do you have any particular memories of training under her?

---

[3] The Dai Nippon Butokukai Bujutsu Senmon Gakko (Greater Japan Martial Virtues Society Martial Arts Training School), commonly referred to as Busen, was founded in 1911 to provide a source of qualified martial arts instructors. Students graduated after completing a course of instruction in techniques, instructional methods, and other cultural aspects pertaining to their particular art and the martial arts in general.

Chiyo Sensei[4] never said much to us, regardless of what we did. Every once in a while, though, she'd say, "Good!" When this happened, we wouldn't even know what she was referring to with this "Good!" I used to think very hard about this when I trained, but finally, in the end, I quit thinking about anything. I was able to do the technique straight. This is what the "Good!" was for. It was not right for the strike to come from the side. It had to come straight down from above. It had to have all the right lines. It took a very long time to get there. I trained over and over again.

In Kyoto, when we went into the dojo, there was a big mirror for training in the changing room. Everyone would stand in front of it to practice. They would look and wonder how do the techniques straight. But I always went where I could train alone. I would do things over and again and would try this or that. Sensei would always know. She would come into the room, which was some distance away, because she hadn't been able to hear my voice. She would ask, "Hanae-san, what are you doing?"

It's like I am always saying: it is not about whose voices you hear. You can say, "That is his voice, that is hers." What is important is whose voices you don't hear. It is with these people that you begin. You, as a teacher, know what kind of training they are doing, or what state of mind they have attained. Of course, I didn't know this at the time. So when Sensei entered the room, I was really surprised. I thought no one would see. But Sensei knew.

My father told me about another example of this kind of awareness. He knew the priest, Nanzenbo, because he practiced Zen for a while. This was when Nanzenbo was quite old, just before his death, in fact. But my father was very impressed by Nanzenbo. When I asked him why, he explained that one day all the monks were sitting as they should be, practicing Zen. But my father was too hot so he went outside of Kaisenji, the temple he was at, and did his Zen sitting on a rock.

[4] Chief naginata teacher at the prewar Butokukai Bujutsu Senmon Gakko.

Later, he went in to talk to Nanzenbo, who, after greetings had been made, asked him, "Where did you practice Zen today?" He could ask this even though he had never left his room. He was too busy for that, because he always had someone coming to see him. But he still knew. My father didn't, at the time, understand how Nanzenbo was able to know this. People just aren't this aware anymore. Only people who've studied or trained for a long time can sense such things. Someone who thinks he is great because of doing four or five years of training really has no idea.

TRADITIONAL WAYS

It is sometimes difficult for foreigners to understand all this. Do you think this is because many elements of traditional Japanese culture are no longer very apparent in modern life?

Yes, that's correct. There is a traditional way of thinking and doing things. For example, in the old days, homes always had a special room that contained a *tokonoma* (decorative alcove) with a hanging scroll and a flower arrangement. This was the place for the guests. You normally spent your time elsewhere. The flowers that were put in the tokonoma were more than just flowers. The arrangement wasn't just a bouquet like you see today. There was a formal way to arrange them.

Then there is the calligraphy. You couldn't hang just any old picture or calligraphy in the tokonoma. It had to be worthy. Now, we live in apartments and people hang all kinds of things all over their walls. But if you go out to rural Japan, you'll still find people who have retained the tradition of keeping scrolls and flower arrangements in the tokonoma.

So, these traditions remain in various individual homes and families. In order to do this, though, you must study flower arrangement. You must do tea ceremony. Martial arts are merely a part of this tradition. You cannot become, or create, a cultivated person without doing all the different things related to the tradition.

You mean in the education or training of people?

Sawada Hanae (right) receiving Tendo-ryu technique at the old Shinjuku Naginata Dojo, ca. 1980.

Yes. When we were in school, everyone also studied the tea ceremony and flower-arranging. I continued studying both of them the entire time I was in Kyoto. Everyone at the Butokukai did. This is called *shitsuke*, breeding or training. Martial arts are one element of shitsuke. People who are fond of the tea ceremony continue their studies and then they teach others. In my family, both my sister and I do naginata, though she has a bad leg now and can't actually practice. Our ancestors did martial arts, so we preserve and continue that tradition, the same as in other martial arts families. But we didn't do only martial arts. We also studied tea ceremony and flower arrangement. You must do many different kinds of things.

The Meaning of Martial Arts Training   45

I'm a woman, so I also needed to know how to cook and sew. When we were younger, we always made our own kimono. We basted them, then put glue on them. We waited for this to dry and then we sewed them. I even embroidered mine. Our children wore clothes that we made ourselves. In the generations before my own, women used to buy silk cocoons, unwind the silk, and then weave it into cloth. They also spun and wove cotton, and then they made clothes for their children out of this. My grandmother did this at my home. These days these sorts of things are cheap, so we all just buy them. But in my time, we all sewed.

Doing the laundry is the same. These days you just dump your clothes in a machine and all of the laundry is washed for you automatically. Before, though, first you had to soak them in plain water. Then you had to fill a barrel with water and wash your clothes in it with soap. Then you had to change the water several times to rinse out the soap. Only then could you say you had done the laundry. Now you just dump it in and it is done.

Rice is the same. Nowadays, you just stick it in the rice cooker and turn on the machine. You can also buy frozen foods and just push a button. Presto… you have curry rice. These things have all become simple… easy. But professional chefs aren't like this. They start by peeling the potatoes and carrots. They start from the very beginning.

These days everything is separate. Restaurants here, laundromats there. Everything has become easy these days. I think perhaps this has made people simple, too. This is what I think, anyway. People have become so simple, it seems they don't understand anything anymore.

WAY OF TEACHING

I was taught a very long time ago by Chiba Sensei, who taught in the Meiji, Taisho, and Showa eras. He would say, "There is a hibachi, right?" Well, actually, let's use the example of this cup, instead. There is a cup here, right? We, the teachers, see the cup from above. Those who can't yet do the techniques see the cup from down here, from the bottom. They don't even know the distance between the bottom and the top. Only those looking down from above can understand certain points. Other people, looking at it from below, cannot really under-stand the shape of the cup or its essence. Therefore, only doing some-thing a little bit in the martial arts does not really mean you have *done* it.

Furthermore, training once or twice a week for ten years or so does not mean you've actually trained for that period of time. If you figure it out, you really have only trained four times a month. Sometimes you miss a class. But, even assuming you came to every lesson, if you count the hours, it still only comes to four times a month, not a full year of practice. So if you practice once a week for ten or twenty years, you haven't really practiced very much. You may not even have practiced for five years, once you add up the actual hours.

So an instructor must be able to perceive a student's actual level, as well as the top and the bottom of the cup?
That is what you must do. Plus, you have to train yourself and pol-ish your skills, over and over again. So, even when you're giving com-mands as you're leading the group, you have to do so as though you're facing each person individually.

Also, the kata, the correct form, must be there. You cannot under-stand it in parts. But you must understand not only the form, but also what is happening in between the forms, the whole time. For example, those people over there are having problems striking the lower leg, so I have them practice just striking the legs. I tell them to strike the shins in different ways and places. But I don't sit just quietly and tell them how to do it. I show them. And when I show them how to do it, I have to do it right. When I show them, I get in there right away, and "Wham!" take the shin. I can do this because I've done it over and over again. It is not something that can be learned right away.

From our perspective as teachers, whatever budo you are talking about, they all have a common thread. We can look at a person and see if he or she is by themselves, looking self-important. If you train with a snobbish attitude, we will see it. If you are training from your heart, we will see that, too. We praise those who work hard by letting them know we know they did just that. Those who say, "I did great today, I am so

The Meaning of Martial Arts Training 47

good at this," receive no praise. We're concerned with the expression of the spirit. Unless you reach that state of mind you will never excel.

You have to be able to both do both parts, *shi* and *uke*, win and lose.[5] You can't do either one alone. You are able to practice because you have a partner. You can't say you are good at it until you can have a kind of spiritual exchange, a give-and-take with your partner. You just think that you are good.

I teach by calling up someone's spirit. Whether I'm teaching them kata or something else, I call up their spirit while I teach. If you don't do it in this way, it never becomes the real thing. It ends up being just a pose.

I have noticed a difference between pre- and postwar martial arts instructors. Not only in training practices, but in thought patterns, too.

Today's instructors are different. You could say they're simply on an escalator. Once they get on it, they automatically get carried upward until they become an instructor. This is not how it worked for us. We had to practice very hard everyday for a very long time until we reached this point.

Only after you have practiced, and practiced hard, every day, morning and night, can you fully appreciate the value of a martial art. You have to train not only when you are here in the dojo, but even when you are home. You have to train always.

WAY OF TRAINING

These days, many instructional books and videos are available. What do you think about people using such things to learn new techniques?

A book will prove or verify what you have already learned; it will help you understand what you can already do. It is not to copy from. You don't look at a book, do the form and then ask what is wrong. You look at the book to show yourself what you've already learned. But it

---

[5] Shi, or doer, is the one who "wins" the technique, while uke, or receiver, usually makes the initial attack and "loses."

48   KORYU BUJUTSU

isn't like that these days. People look at a book, copy the form and say they know how to do it. But this is not budo. It is merely mimicking the forms.

Tendo-ryu focuses on kata practice, but we all also practice atarashii naginata, which includes matches. What is the importance of shiai for martial arts training?

You have to test your forms through these matches. Just doing the forms and saying to yourself, "I did it," isn't enough. I always tell my students that they have to practice the forms and they have to actually strike people in competitive bouts to be able to understand the art. They may practice striking when they train by themselves, but these "attacks" may not actually connect. They won't know this unless they are in a match. They may practice hitting a lot, just by themselves, but they simply can't understand that the form alone is not going to work in a match. Competition very rarely follows form and it's not wise to think that it will.

So, as we do naginata techniques, we go straight forward. In the beginning, we have the fundamentals. You should just go straight forward with these. Your opponents will be alert and you can't depend on them to just stand there while you strike. You have to be able to make split-second decisions and attack based on these decisions. It doesn't do you any good to strike late.

When you train or compete, what should your aim be? One time I came back from a demonstration at Kashima Shrine with you and Kuroda Sensei, and I remember you saying then that the object is not winning, it is "not-losing." I'm not sure what you meant by that. In my case, I don't want to lose. I hate losing. But up until now, I have had very few decent matches. What should I be feeling when I train, when I use the naginata?

You should train by noticing when and where your partner is open. Or about how they are not open at all. You should be thinking about how to strike the opponent where they're open. Matches are *tameshiai*, a mutual testing or trial. You are testing each other.

By testing, you mean testing yourself?

Of course. You aren't there to test the other person. You are doing it to teach yourself. If you want to know what the goal is, it is to become "empty" and to do naginata without actually thinking of anything. This doesn't mean to just stand there and do nothing. But you can't understand this until you do it.

If you don't become empty of desire or conscious thought, you can't do it. Just thinking about how to do something isn't it. Considering how to excel isn't it. It's nothing but doing it over and over, until your spirit enters into it and your body does it naturally, without thinking about anything. It's not something you understand merely by hearing about it. It is something you must do and realize yourself, with your own body. There's no other way.

So I shouldn't be thinking of winning or losing at all?

You hate losing, right? But only through losing can you understand what it means to win. But you only know about winning. You need to lose and then examine your mental state. You have to realize, "Ah, this is what it feels like to lose." Then, you must do the same thing the next time you win. If you don't know what it feels like to both win and lose, then you cannot win. If you can't lose, you can't win. This is a very important thing about martial arts.

In naginata, people are wrong who think they won because they were able to do this technique or that. That is only striking someone. Being able to face your opponent's spirit with your own and then win, though, is not something that's picked up in a mere ten or twenty years of training. It is not an easy thing to do. This is something one understands only after practicing every day for many years.

These days I have one student who is a little bit arrogant, so I am always mad at her. She has no empathy at all for the spirit of her partner. She believes she is superior and acts as if she's the only one who knows anything. This just shows that she can't do it. Unless you and your partner reach the same level, then you can't do the technique properly. You might have good technique, but if you fail to understand the spirit of your partner, then you are doing nothing but the outward form.

When you stand together, you have to help your partner. If you don't help, then your partners will never improve. They will always remain at their current level.

Sawada Hanae (in kimono) teaching at the old Shinjuku Naginata Dojo, ca. 1980.

So you mean, pulling someone up?

Yes. This does not mean only from outside, with the form. Rather, you must pull them up by their spirit, from the inside. The atarashii naginata training method called *hikitate geiko* literally means training to pull or raise someone up. But no one here does that. This is because they are not strong enough. Though they think they're helping to pull each other up, they're really just fighting each other, not helping.

It seems to me that, in the style of aikido that I have practiced, there is an overemphasis on blending, or matching, and not enough concern given to what I suppose one could call "reality" in a combative situation.

When you speak of matching, if your *kokyu*, or breathing, does not match then you do not match. You are thinking merely of form, aren't you? But in order to do *aiki*, both your spirit and that of your partner must enter into play and then come together. When you study aiki, this is what you are studying. What you are doing is not. You think only about winning since you hate to lose. Only by losing, again and again, can you know what it is to win. Aiki can only be understood through repetition. You have to do it over and over, not thinking of your own winning. This is the same thing the student I mentioned above is thinking: "I am strong. Everyone else is no good." This isn't the case. If you can reach the point where both you and your partner become strong together, that's when you'll have something to say. Only then will you understand what is meant when we talk about aiki. "I am strong. Everyone else is no good. I hate losing." This is not martial arts. You only become strong through winning and losing, over and over again.

The martial arts aren't about winning. There's a sort of give-and-take, winning and losing, all thanks to the partner with whom you train. Only through this give-and-take can you excel in budo, can you make progress.

There are people training with children, who sometimes allow the children to hit or throw them, aren't there? If you can't do this, both you and they will never make progress. It's useless if little children think they will always win. So, when you train with children, you must become just like a little child. When they try techniques, this must be accepted and you must react as though you have really been struck or thrown, no matter how small the power. Then this becomes training for you, as well. It is obvious that if you used your full strength you would win against a small child. But you have to allow them to hit you sometimes. You must allow them to be proud of striking you, of winning against you. You must help them build their spirit. Then you will get training, too. And you will become a better martial artist. If you always win, and everyone else always loses, you are not really doing martial arts.

You must train in this manner? For example, in the case of Tendo-ryu, you must perform uke's role with that spirit?

Yes, that's right. It is, then, basically the same as hikitate training. You must look at your partner. When she strikes straight forward, you must be ready for this. If you are afraid and strike out first, this is not training—it in no way pulls the other up to a higher level.

So, as you can see, martial arts are not at all simple. Until you reach that state of mind, where you can train selflessly, you have to study many techniques and principles thoroughly. This involves training with

*Sawada Hanae (right) receiving Abe Tomoko's technique
in a demonstration at Kashima Shrine, ca. 1980.*

many people. To train with only one person is wrong. If just two of
you always train together, you will never be any good.

*So, for example, you shouldn't train only with someone who is your best
training partner? You should train with someone with whom you don't
match well...?*

You must not do the same thing all the time. If you have one thousand people, you have one thousand different partners. All have different spirits. You will learn a great deal by being able to train in the same
way with all one thousand people. That's the kind of thing we are doing in the martial arts. If you can only do it with one person, then you

cannot truly do it. It is the same in kendo, judo, and the other arts as well. In martial arts, one practices winning and losing. You practice again and again, sometimes winning, sometimes losing. This is how you become trained. You are not doing it for others. This is how training happens.

Even the worst people have something that they are good at. Even the tiniest child wants to do his or her best. So you must be able to train even with this tiny child or with this unskilled person. "I won't train with those people because they are no good." This is absolutely not the right attitude.

You must avoid having a hard heart and thinking that you alone are skilled. If you possess a heart that is hard like this, you are in trouble. You will make no progress. You must always have a free spirit. Everyone is different.

If you can't do the kata with anyone and everyone, then you're not really doing the form. If you practice earnestly, eventually you'll come to understand whether you are more or less skilled than your opponent. If you always try to be the strong one, if you're a braggart, then you will not improve. *Kokoro*, or spirit, is difficult to understand, not simple at all. Even with Zen, there are some people who understand right away and some that never comprehend it. The same holds true for naginata. Some people grasp it right away. Others never make it that far because they aren't really practicing. If you don't practice, you can't make it that far. Just because you are able to talk about it means only that you can put it into words, it does not mean that you have actually trained.

If people don't take corrections and then try to integrate them into their training, then they have no meaning. Just because they try it a few times doesn't mean they can do it. So, as you see, training is not a simple thing. You never reach a state where everything is right. You do something a couple of times, and you may even feel good about it. But unless you have practiced something a thousand times, you cannot really say that you've done it. If you can't do it the same way a thousand times, then you aren't really able to do it.

For example, Niwata Sensei, the iaido teacher, took the *hachidan* exam for years without passing. Then, one day he went in and passed the exam. Once he passed, he couldn't believe what a simple thing it was that he hadn't understood. He understood because he had finally reached the state of mind necessary to see. You train in order to attain this state of mind. And this can't be taught.

My younger brother's wife is doing calligraphy. She recently told me it was getting difficult and she was considering quitting. I told her, "You are planning to quit at the most important part of your training. How long has it taken you to reach this stage?" "It has taken a long time." "Why would you quit now? Now, when you are at the point where you are finally able to learn the more important parts of your art?" If she quits, all her training to this point, between ten and twenty years, would go to waste.

Would you please say a little more about the idea of training with a "pure spirit" and how one ought to practice?

When you're doing your art, you have to make your spirit pure. You must not be concerned about whether people are watching or not, whether your junior is paying attention, whether you are teaching correctly. All of that is unimportant.

Martial arts are not for merely showing off the forms. One is supposed to do them from the heart. But if I speak of this heart, this spirit of the martial arts, it's difficult to understand what I'm talking about. People who don't train, can't understand.

If there are desires, it's no good. It takes years to get rid of desire. People have desires in their heart. If I do this, will I look good? Will it go well, if I do this? They think about lots of things. The more you think, the more you end up running around in circles. In order to reach this desire-free state, you have to have attained a certain state of mind. Without reaching the state of a pure spirit, you cannot progress in martial arts. You cannot show that you have reached this state unless you truly have. People training are all making the same movements. But it shows when someone has a pure spirit. We can see it. We notice this achievement and think to ourselves, "He has finally become serious, he has finally attained the necessary state of mind." People might come up and tell us how much they have learned, how well they have performed. But when we look at them, we know. We think to ourselves, they just haven't got it yet, have they? You can only see this when you have become capable of looking from above, from this state of mind, as I explained earlier with the example of the cup. You can't see it from below.

This is a bit of an odd question, but what is your objective in training? After all, there is now no one above you.

My objective is to train with young people while maintaining the proper spirit. That is why, when I practice with others in Tendo-ryu, I tell them to cut straight and true, and I will do the same. I can't tell them what to do unless I am doing it first. I also have to do it with a pure and proper spirit. When you practice with somebody else, you must do so with the proper spirit. Then you can raise yourself to a higher level. It's not something to be done only for appearances, so that you look good, or so that you don't get hit by the other person. You have to train over and again. It's like I was telling you earlier: we are looking from above, so we can see what you are thinking about quite easily. We know the shape of the cup. If it is a big cup, we know that. If it is small, we know that, too. We are looking from above, thus we see it all. To attain this state of mind takes a very long time.

I was talking earlier about my teacher, Chiba Sensei. He wrote the most beautiful calligraphy. I would never tell him this directly, though. I once said to his wife, "Chiba Sensei's writing is so beautiful, when I look at it gives me a feeling I can't explain. There are some places where the characters are delicate and thin and other places where they are very strong. But, over all, there is an incredibly beautiful balance. The paper he chooses is just right. There's something in his calligraphy that goes straight to my heart. It stills my soul. It makes me feel quite calm, that the world is beautiful. When I look at such things I wonder at their beauty and wish that I, too, could achieve that kind of spirit." His wife, who has since passed away, commented, "Hanae-san, I didn't know you thought about such things." I replied, "When I look at something like Chiba Sensei's calligraphy, I can't even explain how beautiful I feel inside. It can only be described as beautiful."

Dolls are the same. All dolls are different. A beautiful doll is one that emanates the spirit of the person who created it. A doll artist does not think to himself, "Now, I'll make a beautiful doll." Rather, he makes it with a pure, beautiful spirit. The outcome is thus this beautiful doll. Without this pure spirit, it isn't possible. If he worries about whether or not the doll will sell, or whether it will be appreciated, the doll will not be beautiful. Nothing created with these kinds of questions in mind can be beautiful. That is the difficult part of spirit: it is a thing you can't show others.

Sawada Hanae receiving technique in a demonstration at the Shubukan Dojo, Itami City, 1996.

The Meaning of Martial Arts Training

Diane Skoss attended her first classical martial arts demonstration at the Nippon Budokan on Valentine's Day in 1988. Since then she's watched, photographed, videotaped, and, as a member of the Toda-ha Buko-ryu, participated in numerous Kobudo Shinkokai and Kobudo Kyokai demonstrations throughout Japan.

Field Guide to the Classical Japanese Martial Arts

Diane Skoss

Introduction

Sitting through an entire day of *koryu bujutsu* demonstrations can be a very tiring and bewildering experience. The programs (at least in Japan, where you are most likely to have such an opportunity) are written in Japanese, and often, unless you know one of the participants, it's difficult to distinguish one tradition from the next. I realized early on that if I were ever to get anything substantial out of these demonstrations, I'd have to come up with some sort of system for identifying each *ryu*. At first, the scrawls in my programs referred mostly to people I knew ("Muto Sensei does Yagyu Shingan-ryu"), or unusual weapons ("The school with the ultra-long naginata is Chokugen-ryu"), or distinctive clothing ("The girls in *furisode* kimono are doing Yoshin-ryu"), or weird techniques ("Jigen-ryu is the one with the crazy granny technique"). While the nature of these notes has evolved over the years, their usefulness has continued.

Several years ago I had the good fortune to meet a very talented professional photographer, Inoue Kazuhiro. He came to the annual kobudo demonstration at Meiji Shrine and shot rolls and rolls of the most stunning slides—among them the photo on the cover of this book. The minute I saw Inoue-san's photographs, I knew I had found the right partners for my little "cheat-sheets," and the "Field Guide to the Classical Japanese Martial Arts" was born. I've supplemented each entry with information gleaned from the major Japanese written sources on the classical *ryuha* (listed below), and added some additional photographs accumulated by Meik and me.

I've selected the first twelve ryu for this series (to be continued in further publications, should this book prove sufficiently popular) based entirely on the quality of the photographs I had available. There are many classical martial traditions still practiced in Japan—all are worthy to be chronicled, and I hope to gradually collect material to showcase as many of them as possible. It's also important to realize that there are often several lines of a particular school; I've included information on the line that I know best. This does not mean that other lines are not equally legitimate or active.

References

International Hoplology Society. 1992. *The IHS Guide to Classical Martial Ryu of Japan, No. 1.* Kamuela, Hawaii: International Hoplology Society.

Japan: An Illustrated Encyclopedia. 1994. Tokyo: Kodansha.

Miyazaki, M., ed. 1994. *Nihon Densho Bugei Ryuha: Dokuhon* (Japanese Traditional Martial Arts Schools: A Handbook). Tokyo: Shin Jimbutsu Oraisha.

Nihon Kobudo Kyokai. 1997. *Dai Nijukai Zen Nihon Kobudo Embu Taikai* (Twentieth Annual All-Japan Classical Martial Arts Demonstration). Tokyo: Nippon Budokan.

Nihon Kobudo Shinkokai. 1990. *Nihon Kobudo Taikai: Nihon Kobudo Shinkokai Soritsu Gojugoshunen Kinenshi* (A Gathering of Japanese Classical Martial Arts: 55th Anniversary of the Nihon Kobudo Shinkokai). Tokyo: Nihon Kobudo Shinkokai.

Nihon Kobudo Shinkokai. 1995. *Nihon Kobudo Taikai: Nihon Kobudo Shinkokai Soritsu Rokujushunen Kinenshi* (A Gathering of Japanese Classical Martial Arts: 60th Anniversary of the Nihon Kobudo Shinkokai). Tokyo: Nihon Kobudo Shinkokai.

Warner, G. and D.F. Draeger. 1982. *Japanese Swordsmanship: Technique and Practice.* New York and Tokyo: Weatherhill.

Watatani, K. and T. Yamada. 1978. *Bugei Ryuha Daijiten* (Dictionary of Japanese Martial Art Traditions). Tokyo: Tokyo Kopii Shuppanbu.

KORYU BUJUTSU

ASAYAMA ICHIDEN-RYU HEIHO
浅山一伝流兵法

Weapons/systems: kenjutsu, iaijutsu, kamajutsu, bojutsu, taijutsu
Date founded: Tensho (1573-1593) or Keicho (1596-1615)
Founder: Asayama Ichidensai Shigetatsu
Present representative: Ozaki Kiyoshi
Prefecture: Kanagawa

Field notes: The *iai* techniques of Asayama Ichiden-ryu are all practiced in paired forms; there is no solo sword-drawing. The *kama* used in this tradition is huge, with a long wide blade. Practitioners today wear unusual trouser-like *hakama,* because, according to Matsui Kenji (pictured at left), Asayama Ichiden-ryu is a bujutsu of the *goshi* (farmer-warrior or landed *bushi*).

KORYU BUJUTSU

Hyoho Niten Ichi-ryu

KENJUTSU

兵法二天一流剣術

Weapons/systems: kenjutsu *(odachi, kodachi, nitto)*
Date founded: first half of seventeenth century
Founder: Miyamoto Musashi Fujiwara Genshin, 1584-1645
Present headmaster: 10th soke Imai Masayuki
Prefecture: Oita

Field notes: Niten Ichi-ryu founder Miyamoto Musashi was perhaps the most famous of all Japanese swordsmen. He survived some sixty matches during the course of his life, and was the author of *Gorin no sho* (The Book of Five Rings), as well as a famous artist. The first two characters of the school's name, which are usually pronounced *heiho* in Japanese, are in this tradition pronounced *hyoho*.

Niten Ichi-ryu techniques are economical, with no flashy or exaggerated movements. Targeting is precise, and the distancing and timing of techniques is exceptionally tight and without wasted motion. This school is most noted for its series of five two-sword techniques, but there are also twelve single sword forms and seven short sword forms.

KASHIMA SHINDEN
JIKISHINKAGE-RYU KENJUTSU
鹿島神伝直心影流剣術

Weapons/systems: kenjutsu *(odachi, kodachi)*
Date founded: late fifteenth or early sixteenth century
Founder: Matsumoto Bizen-no-Kami Naokatsu, 1467-1524
Present headmaster: No single recognized headmaster; the current
representative of the Odani-ha is Iwasa Masaru.
Prefecture: Chiba

Field notes: Jikishinkage-ryu, as this school is known for short, has its
origins in the martial arts practiced at the Kashima Shrine; it was initially known as Kashima Shinden-ryu.

A variety of different types of practice weapons are used, including
an extremely heavy *furibo* and an especially large *bokuto* used in a set
called *hojo,* for spiritual and stamina training. The Jikishinkage-ryu also
uses a *fukuro shinai* (leather-covered bamboo practice weapon) and
habiki, a metal sword, often a live blade. Short sword techniques are
unusual in that the weapon is wielded with two hands.

Jikishinkage-ryu techniques often appear to be very simple, but in
fact employ extremely sophisticated *kokyu* (breathing) and *kiai* (focusing verbalizations), with the goal of psychologically dominating an opponent. A particularly unusual technique, with both practitioners
ending up standing on one leg, is usually demonstrated with live blades
and focuses on precise distancing and superb body control.

KORYU BUJUTSU

KURAMA-RYU KENJUTSU
鞍馬流剣術

Weapons/systems: kenjutsu *(odachi)*
Date founded: Tensho (1573-1593)
Founder: Ono Shokan
Present headmaster: 17th soke Shibata Tetsuo
Prefecture: Tokyo

Field notes: The techniques of the Kurama-ryu are characterized by frequent use of *uchiotoshi,* cutting straight through the opponent's sword. The special set of sword techniques formulated for the police during the Meiji period, Keishicho-ryu, includes Kurama-ryu technique. Shibata family members have been prominent sword instructors for the Imperial guards and the police for over one hundred years.

Koryu Bujutsu

Maniwa Nen-ryu
馬庭念流

Weapons/systems: kenjutsu *(odachi),*
naginatajutsu, sojutsu, yadomejutsu
Date founded: 1368
Founder: Soma Shiro Yoshimoto, later known as Nen Ami Jion
Present headmaster: Since the death of 24th soke Higuchi Sadahiro in
1995, the school has been led by the Maniwa Nen-ryu Hozonkai, under
the direction of the Higuchi family.
Prefecture: Gunma, Maniwa Village

Field notes: Nen-ryu is one of the oldest surviving traditions of swordsmanship in Japan. Initially formulated by Nen Ami Jion in the fourteenth century, Higuchi Kaneshige took this art to Maniwa in 1494.
Maniwa Nen-ryu has never been attached to a particular domain, and
instead has always been affiliated with the village as a means of defense.
Noted for very strong swordsmen throughout history, who fought and
won many bouts with famous swordsmen of other schools.

Maniwa Nen-ryu includes extremely strong *kokyu* and *kiai* training;
the seemingly clumsy footwork and postures look awkward to the uninitiated, but actually contain a great deal of subtle technique. Nen-ryu
kiriwari jiai training employs the *fukuro shinai,* quilted gauntlet, and
padded headgear for protection so that practitioners can engage in
matches to test their skills. Techniques of this tradition work against
both armored and unarmored opponents.

MORISHIGE-RYU HOJUTSU
森重流砲術

Weapons/systems: hojutsu *(hinawaju)*
Date founded: 1803
Founder: Morishige Yukie Tsuyoshi
Present representative: Shimazu Kenji
Prefecture: Kanagawa

Field notes: Morishige-ryu presents a colorful (and noisy) demonstration, with participants in full armor, complete with banners. This school teaches seven basic firing positions, as well as a number of different forms for firing under various conditions, including, for example, how to load the musket when crossing a body of water. The *hinawaju,* or matchlock musket, used in this tradition has not changed in design since the mid-sixteenth century.

This firearm, originally based on the Portuguese harquebus, was an essential key to the unification of Japan. The use of such firearms allowed Oda Nobunaga and Takeda Shingen to revolutionize Japanese military strategy.

Owari Kan-ryu sojutsu
尾張貫流槍術

Weapons/systems: sojutsu *(kuda yari, su yari),*
kenjutsu *(odachi, kodachi)*
Date founded: 1671
Founder: Tsuda Gonnojo Taira Nobuyuki, 1654-1698
Present representative: 8th generation inheritor Kato Isao
Prefecture: Aichi

Field notes: Gonnojo, who was the son of a retainer of the Owari do-main, studied Ito-ryu *kuda yari* under Mori Kanbe'e and Saburi-ryu *sojutsu* under Saburi Enyuemon Tadamura before creating his own style of spearsmanship. Kan-ryu, sometimes called Tsuda-ryu or Tsuda Kan-ryu, was adopted as an "official" style of the Owari domain by its 4th lord, Tokugawa Yoshimichi.

One of the most distinctive features is the use of the kuda yari, which is quite long; the kuda or sleeve allows the spearsman to change the *maai* very rapidly and to make effective use of the spear's full length. Unlike in most sojutsu traditions, techniques can be practiced using either a right- or left-sided stance. Also, unlike most other koryu, training begins with *shiai* and ends with *kata.* Shiai training is done wearing protective equipment similar to that of modern jukendo.

Koryu Bujutsu

SHINGYOTO-RYU KENJUTSU
心形刀流剣術

Weapons/systems: kenjutsu *(odachi, kodachi, nitto),* iaijutsu,
naginatajutsu *(kagitsuki naginata)*
Date founded: 1682
Founder: Iba Josuiken Hideaki
Present head instructor: Kobayashi Masao (featured on the cover, and
pictured left), 5th generation instructor at the Kameyama Enbujo
Prefecture: Mie

Field notes: The meaning of the name Shingyoto-ryu is considered to
be particularly significant: when one has trained sufficiently with a
sword one gains sublime skills—the heart/spirit/mind (*shin*) gives rise
to form (*gyo*), which is manifested by the use of the sword (*to*). The
way you perform technique arises from your spirit and intent. If the
spirit is correct, the technique will be correct; if the cultivation of spirit
is insufficient, the technique will be distorted.

Shingyoto-ryu is notable for the variety of its techniques, which include a series called *makuragatana,* or bedside sword. The use of the
sword in this school is characterized by compact movements and frequent use of body displacement. It also one of two known schools to
use a *kagistuki naginata,* or naginata with an iron cross bar.

The Kameyama Enbujo, where this school is based, is perched atop
an imposing castle wall; it was the dojo located on the Kameyama castle
grounds for use by domainal retainers. It burned to the ground in the
mid-1980s but has been reconstructed in an exact, though slightly
larger, replica.

KORYU BUJUTSU

Shinmuso
Hayashizaki-ryu iaijutsu
神夢想林崎流抜刀術

Weapons/systems: iaijutsu *(odachi, kodachi)*
Date founded: late sixteenth century
Founder: Hayashizaki Jinsuke Shigenobu, ca. 1542-1621
Present representative: Sasamori Takemi, *menkyo kaiden*
Prefecture: Tokyo

Field notes: Hayashizaki-ryu is considered by some to be the oldest school of batto/iaijutsu. Two lines diverged at the time of the 5th headmaster (a number of schools of iaido also trace their roots to Hayashizaki Jinsuke); the other survives as Hayashizaki Muso-ryu in Yamagata Prefecture. The line which became Shinmuso Hayashizaki-ryu was adopted by Tsugaru Nobumasa, lord of the Tsugaru domain, as an official style of his clan.

Techniques include seated paired sword-drawing, as well as solo *iai*. They are characterized by frequent use of *jumonji* (control by crossing the enemy's attack), and *yoko ichimonji* (horizontal draw and cut covering action), and are practiced against attackers coming from a variety of directions. The blade of the sword used in the Hayashizaki-ryu is nearly one meter long (although it is a short sword technique pictured at left).

KORYU BUJUTSU

Tendo-ryu naginatajutsu
天道流薙刀術

Weapons/systems: naginatajutsu, kenjutsu (*odachi, kodachi, nitto, tanto, kaiken*), jojutsu (broken *naginata*), kusarigamajutsu
Date founded: November 21, 1582
Founder: Saito Hangan Denkibo Katsuhide
Present headmaster: 16th soke Mitamura Takeko
Prefecture: Kyoto

Field notes: Tendo-ryu founder Denkibo was from Ibaragi, and studied Kashima Shinto-ryu under Tsukahara Bokuden. On the last of one hundred days of *shugyo* and prayer at Kamakura Tsurugaoka Hachimangu, Denkibo dreamed that he had received a scroll explaining *makoto no michi*, the way of sincerity. This he interpreted to mean the way of heaven, so he christened his art Ten-ryu, tradition of heaven. It later came to be known as Tendo-ryu, way of heaven tradition.

In Tendo-ryu kata is performed as if it were real combat. One moves always in response to the opponent's movements, and applies logical techniques. Most characteristic techniques include *egurizuki,* which is a stretching, spiraling, binding thrust. Also distinctive is *kasaneuchi,* "piling on" or striking from above, done by crossing the feet, unwinding and using the power of the hips; *kuruma,* circular slashing movements; and *kozui ken,* cutting to the bone marrow.

Koryu Bujutsu

YAGYU SHINGAN-RYU TAIJUTSU
柳生心眼流体術

Weapons/systems: taijutsu (jujutsu), kenjutsu, bojutsu,
naginatajutsu, iaijutsu
Date founded: early 1600s
Founder: Araki Mataemon, 1584-1637
Present headmaster: 11th soke Kajitsuka Yasushi
Prefecture: Kanagawa

Field notes: Founder Araki Mataemon trained under Yagyu Munenori
of the Yagyu Shinkage-ryu, and was granted permission to use the
Yagyu name in his own school's name by Yagyu Jubei. "Shingan" refers
to seeing with both the eyes and the mind or spirit.

Yagyu Shingan-ryu includes both armored and unarmored combat
techniques and strategies. It is a comprehensive system, starting with
taijutsu to form body and spirit, followed by weapons training. The
bojutsu is quite strong, and uses a characteristic movement in which
the two bo are slammed or clacked together (shown demonstrated by
Muto Masao at left). Practitioners wear white headbands, which are
supposed to contain iron plates for simple head protection.

KORYU BUJUTSU

Yagyu Shinkage-ryu hyoho
柳生新陰流兵法

Weapons/systems: kenjutsu *(odachi, kodachi, nitto)*
Date founded: Muromachi period, ca. 1658
Founder: Kamiizumi Ise-no-Kami Nobutsuna, 1508-1578; the Yagyu
line was founded by Yagyu Sekishusai Munetoshi, 1527-1606
Present headmaster: 22st soke Yagyu Koichi
Prefecture: Aichi

Field notes: Kamiizumi Ise-no-Kami, who had trained in both Kashima and Katori Shinto-ryu, created Shinkage-ryu based on Kage-ryu, which he learned from its founder Aisu Ikkosai. Yagyu Sekishusai began to train under Kamiizumi after being soundly defeated by one of his students. Together with his son Munenori, Yagyu Sekishusai introduced Yagyu Shinkage-ryu to Tokugawa Ieyasu, whereupon the school became the official school of the Tokugawa family, and Munenori became Ieyasu's personal instructor.

Shinkage-ryu was probably the first school to use *fukuro shinai*, developed by Kamiizumi as a training device to allow full impact without injury.

In addition to the techniques of the *honden,* which descend directly from Kamiizumi, there are also *gaiden* techniques, added later by various masters. In the Owari line there is also a series of jo techniques known as Jubei no jo, as well as a more recently developed set of batto techniques, Yagyu Seigo-ryu battojutsu.

David A. Hall, who holds a doctorate in Buddhist Studies and Military History from UC Berkeley, has extensive experience in the classical martial arts as well as being an ordained Tendai Buddhist priest. As part of his esoteric training, he has actually practiced some of the Marishiten-related rituals that he mentions in this chapter. During his fourteen years in Japan, Hall began his training in the Shindo Muso-ryu, Kashima Shinden Jikishinkage-ryu, and the Yagyu Shinkage-ryu.

MARISHITEN
BUDDHIST INFLUENCES ON COMBATIVE BEHAVIOR

David A. Hall

INTRODUCTION

Buddhism has had a long relationship with combat and warriors, a somewhat ironic association since Buddhism is aimed at ending suffering, and combat is essentially a manifestation of violent behavior. However, neither Buddhism nor combative behavior are one-dimensional entities. Buddhism has been able to accommodate combatants in its fold in order to lead them toward its highest ideals, and combatants have adapted much from Buddhism, becoming more compassionate in the process.

In fact, one Buddhist-oriented military cult has flourished in various parts of Asia since the fifth century A.D., and it is still practiced in Japan among serious practitioners of the military, police, and classical-warrior disciplines. The central figure of the cult is a goddess of the Buddhist pantheon, referred to in Japanese as Marishiten.[1] She was the patron goddess of the Japanese warrior class for over nine hundred years and has since been an important figure for various groups of people—modern military personnel and police officers, members of elite classical warrior traditions, sumo wrestlers, members of various religious traditions, and others. In the Buddhist texts devoted to her, the goddess' combative powers are described as follows:

---

[1] Marishiten (<Sanskrit-*Mârîcî(devî)* or *Mârîcî(devatâ)* <Chinese-*Molichihtian*) is sometimes depicted as male. However, in most texts she is described as a goddess, and I have, thus, consistently referred to her as female.

No one can see her, no one can know her, no one can seize her, no one can harm her, no one can deceive her, no one can fetter her, no one can cloud her mind, and she does not bear malice.

Marishiten is also described as being selfless and compassionate, a protectress of sentient beings facing a variety of calamities, and as a bodhisattva.

Development of the Buddhist Mârîcî

As Mahâyâna Buddhism began its spread across Asia during the first and second centuries a.d., it began to evolve and embrace new philosophical teachings as well as expanding its pantheon of Buddhas and bodhisattvas. The eclectic Buddhist schools of the mid-first millennium a.d. not only began to deify magical spells[2] but also began to incorporate local divinities and their cult practices into Buddhism. This process continued throughout Buddhism's spread across Asia.

The *tantras*,[3] the texts of these new schools, include an array of Buddhisized Hindu gods, goddesses, and spirits, sometimes only thinly covered by a Buddhist veneer. These early tantras were essentially books of spells, known as *dhâranîsûtras*. Attributed to Sâkyamuni, the original Buddha, they were accepted by the Buddhist community in order to allow non-Buddhists to join while continuing to follow the cults of their own deities. One of these new Buddhist cults was that of the goddess Mârîcî. The origins of the goddess are obscure, but she appears to be a tantric Buddhist amalgamation of several Brâhmanical, Iranian, and non-Aryan antecedents. Significantly, a number of *siddhi* (supernatural powers), such as invisibility and the ability to confuse enemies—frequently mentioned in Buddhist Mârîcî texts—were also characteristics

[2] For a description of this process, see *Marishiten: Buddhism and the Warrior Goddess* (Hall 1990, 30-44).

[3] A tantra is a Buddhist ritual text focused on the cult of a deity.

of Mârîcî's Indian predecessors: Indra, the Brâhmanic Marîci, and the Maruts. Marishiten's siddhi, especially those of a combative nature, became more prominent as the cult evolved and later dhâranîsftras devoted to her were composed.

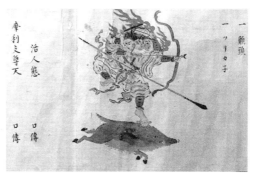

Boar-mounted Marishiten from a Yoshin-ryu scroll dated 1758. Muto Masao collection.

The Buddhist cult of Marishiten appeared in China by the early sixth century where, over a period of several hundred years, it evolved and was adapted to the needs of the military Taoist sects.[4] By the eighth century, the texts of the Marishiten cult were available in Japan where the goddess soon became the patron deity of the rising warrior class. In Japan, we find a wealth of literature on Marishiten produced by both Buddhist priests and warriors, as well as living testimony to the importance of the cult among present-day combatants and exponents of the koryu bujutsu.

MARISHITEN'S IMPORTANCE TO THE JAPANESE WARRIOR

Marishiten's popularity among Japanese warriors was primarily due to the particular synergy of combative powers with which the goddess was thought to empower her devotees: invisibility, the ability to confuse enemies, clarity of mind, intuition, imperturbability, selflessness and, ultimately, compassion.

---

[4] In China, Mârîcî (Molichitian) was also called Tou-mu, the Mother of the Dipper, or Tou-lao, the Goddess of the North Star. In Taoist texts she became an important figure in the military Taoism of Wu-tang Shan.

In Japan, the cult of Marishiten and the use of related combative esoterica such as the *kuji* had become popular with the Japanese warrior at least by the thirteenth century, as evidenced by a reference in a letter by the monk Nichiren. Although this letter does not mention the specific combative siddhi or miraculous powers attributed to Marishiten, we do find a direct reference concerning Marishiten's powers of invisibility and confusion in the fourteenth century war tale known as the *Taiheiki*.[5] In this text, the Prince of the Great Pagoda covers himself with Buddhist *sûtras* and silently recites a spell of invisibility in order to hide himself from a band of enemy warriors. The warriors are unable to locate the prince, and as they depart, the prince notes that he has been saved by the "invisible" or "unseen" workings of Marishiten and the Sixteen Good Deities (Yamashita 1972, 1:220-221).

This section of the *Taiheiki* was evidently composed sometime around the fourth decade of the fourteenth century. At about this same time, the well-known warrior, Kusunoki Masashige, was displaying battle flags of the *sansenjin* (three war *kami*)—Fudo Myoo, Aizen Myoo, and Marishiten.[6] Also during the mid-fourteenth century, we begin to find Marishiten's power of invisibility being applied to martial use in such texts on battlefield strategy as the *Heiho Reizuisho* (1359; Ishioka and Arima 1967, 18).

INVISIBILITY

Marishiten's association with invisibility—her primary attribute—dates from her earliest origins and is prominent in Japanese warrior literature from at least the thirteenth century onward. However, it is difficult to imagine, from a twentieth century perspective, just what sort of powers of invisibility these references indicate. One possibility is

---

[5] The *Taiheiki* is a war tale concerned with events in early fourteenth century Japan. This reference can be found in chapter five of McCullough's translation, *The Taiheiki: A Chronicle of Medieval Japan*.

[6] Sasama Yoshihiko, interview with the author, Kamakura, Japan, 12 April 1988. See also Sasama (1987, 817-818) for a description of the sansenjin and an illustration of Kusunoki's banner.

that they refer to the obfuscation of intent in strategic and tactical troop movement. In other words, a *gunbaisha* (practitioner of battle-field divination) may have seen himself as deriving his powers of divination from Marishiten and/or concealed his tactical intentions or troop movements from his enemy via a war fan protected by Marishiten's power of invisibility.

On a more personal level, it may well have been the sleight-of-hand or disappearing-act sort of invisibility for which the Japanese *ninja* (mercenary specialists in espionage) in later centuries became famous—at least in the popular literature. Mention should also be made here of another type of invisibility indicated in one of the original nuances of the term ninja. The first character in this compound is *shinobi* (endurance). In this context, a ninja—like the mole of modern espionage—might be planted in a certain location for a number of years before being called upon to supply information. In this way he or she was invisible.

However, warrior invisibility was something different. In contrast to the ninja, Japanese warriors of the Heian, Kamakura, and early Muromachi periods did not rely on camouflage coloration or other techniques to hide themselves from enemies on the battlefield. In fact, it appears from reading war tales such as the *Heike Monogatari, Taiheiki,* and so on, that the warrior, once on the field, made every effort to be seen! This was especially true in the late Heian period when warriors shouted out challenges to each other before engaging in battle.[7] The armor of those eras also reveals a complete lack of concern for concealment in both design and coloration. Indeed, such works as the

---

[7] There are numerous references to this. For example, see book 9, Chapter 2, "Race at the Uji River" and chapter 3, "Battle on the River Bank," in *The Tale of the Heike* (Kitagawa and Tsuchida 1975, 511-518). Also see Draeger and Smith (1969, 83).

Heike Monogatari devote a good deal of space to describing how colorfully each combatant was dressed.

It might be argued that concealment[8] is of questionable use to mounted swordsmen going out to meet opponents. This is, of course, true. However, the classical Japanese warrior also depended heavily on the bow and arrow; a common term for warriorship in medieval Japan was *kyuba no michi,* the "way of the bow and horse." The bow is a missile weapon and, like a firearm, can be used from a concealed position. Japanese history reveals, however, that this weapon was also used out in the open, both for tactical purposes and as a demonstration of courage in facing an opponent "man-to-man."

During that period, the warrior had to become accomplished in the proper shooting posture known as *yugamae.* Mastering this posture was essential so that on the battlefield it would facilitate the warrior's psycho-physical dominance[9] over his opponent before, during, and after firing his weapon. This psycho-physical dominance is not a dominance of physical strength, rather it is a psychological dominance and control of an opponent expressed through body language—eye contact, posture, breathing, movement, etc. As we shall see, the combative "powers" required to create and maintain this dominance—whether the warrior was using a sword, bow and arrow, or other weapon—are those same combative siddhi idealized in Marishiten.

Since the warrior ethos of the time precluded hiding as a legitimate battlefield tactic, what then was this Marishiten-derived invisibility that was not only efficacious but acceptable in the sociocultural climate of the early Japanese warrior class? To throw some light on what invisibil-

---

[8] I use this term here in contrast to cover, which protects one from hostile fire but does not necessarily "conceal." Concealment hides you from view but does not necessarily protect you from fire.

[9] This is referred to by a variety of terms by the Japanese including *zanshin* (remaining awareness [form]), *kiai* (spirit unification), yugamae (posture [necessary for firing the] bow), etc. For want of a better exact English equivalent, I have resorted to the rather contrived term "psycho-physical dominance."

ity and other combative siddhi might actually have been to Japanese warriors on the battlefield, it is useful to call upon current hoplological[10] research into combative psychology.

The Biological Basis of Combative Siddhi

Over the past twenty years much research has been carried out in fields concerned with the nature of combative behavior and performance, the majority of which has been in the areas of cultural anthropology, biomechanics, and psychology. Especially significant in the context of this investigation are studies carried out by socio-biologist E.O. Wilson, ethologist Irenäus Eibl-Eibesfeldt (a leading scholar in the study of animal aggression and its application in the human context), hoplologist Richard Hayes (a leader in the development of a comprehensive matrix of combative adaptive traits), hoplologists Donn F. Draeger, Hunter B. Armstrong, and myself (research in combative behavior and performance), behavioral psychologist Hans Selye (pioneer in the areas of human psycho-physical response to stress), and psychologist Laurie Hamilton (specialist in the area of combative psychology). The frameworks these researchers have devised are useful in attempting to understand what the Japanese warrior was referring to by *ongyoho, majutsu,* (both terms for invisibility) and other powers attributed to Marishiten.

Traditional Japanese Tantric Buddhist views credit accomplishment in human psycho-physical performance to a synergy of body, speech, and mind. Modern analytical approaches attempt to investigate more deeply and delineate more clearly these three aspects of human "being." Hayes has proposed eight genotypical combative traits in three categories—brain-bound (mind), body-bound, and action-bound. Although extrapolated from Japanese combative culture, Hayes' traits are also

---

[10] Hoplology is a term coined by the explorer Sir Richard Burton during the nineteenth century. Its modern definition was created by Donn F. Draeger, founder of the IHS in the 1970s, and has since been expanded to include the study of combative behavior, performance, and systems.

useful in evaluating combative behavior in areas outside of Japan. Three of these traits are of particular interest here because they are psycho-physical in nature. These are steadfast/imperturbable mind, cognition/intuition, and volition. Of secondary concern here are his three "body-bound" traits—omnipoise, abdominal, and respiratory/vocality—and two "action-bound" traits—force/yield and synchronous.

Focusing on the manifestation of survival-oriented mental and physical behaviors that have been observed in combative situations, let's look briefly at the functional nature of these three psycho-physical combative traits.

STEADFAST/IMPERTURBABLE MIND

When the five senses (sight, hearing, touch, smell, taste) register threat, that threat is cognitively perceived and/or intuitively apprehended by the brain through processing by both the left and right brain hemispheres. The psycho-physical system then responds with what Hans Selye has termed the general adaptation syndrome or GAS (1974). Selye's hypothesis describes the GAS in three stages: an alarm reaction, a resistance stage, and an extinction stage. He further divides the alarm reaction into two phases, a shock phase and a counter-shock phase. In the counter-shock phase the body's sympathetic nervous system is aroused by the release of pituitary and adrenocortical hormones. This process helps prepare the organism for "fight or flight," the response to an attack in which the individual either defends itself or flees.[11] In the resistance stage, continued protection against stress is provided through the production of corticosteroid and the sympathetic system then re-

---

[11] It is important to note that "fight or flight" is not the only response to danger/threat. There is also the "freeze" response in which the individual may intentionally halt movement to avoid detection or become paralyzed, unable to move. Examinations of this general inhibitory syndrome can be found in *Hoplology Theoretics—Vol. I: Conceptual Tools for the Hoplologist* (Hayes and Draeger 1984), and "Fight, Flight or Freeze: Implications of the Passive Fear Response for Anxiety and Depression" (Hamilton 1989). See also *The Naked Ape* (Morris 1967, 128-163), for more detail on fight or flight.

turns to a normal level of excitement. If stress is too prolonged, the extinction stage may occur as the body's protective mechanisms break down and the organism enters a state of collapse.

However, before the alarm reaction sets the general adaptation syndrome into motion, it may be controlled or completely stopped by the brain's production of hormones that can inhibit the GAS in specific parts of the body, completely or in part (Hayes 1989). If the alarm reaction is partially or completely blocked in a context in which the cognitive/intuitive functions are in command, we may refer to these states respectively as steadfast mind and imperturbable mind.[12] Inability to block the alarm reaction results in anxiety, fear, panic or, in some cases, mindless rage. Although the general adaptation syndrome may be adaptive in short-term, fight or flight situations, it is maladaptive for protracted periods of combat because it uses up energy reserves and may quickly result in collapse or even death. There are, in fact, many accounts of this in the annals of personal combat. For example, H.R. Ellis Davidson, paraphrasing an old Irish epic called the *Táin*, notes that battle fury (which is one extreme of alarm reaction) among the Celts was sometimes "so violent that some men died before the fighting began" (Davidson 1988, 98).

The epitome of warriorship in a number of cultures, including Japan, however, was to be cool, calm, collected, and deadly. This obviously requires an ability to block the alarm reaction: to be active, on the run, and still conserve energy, apply internalized technique, solve prob-

---

[12] Imperturbable mind is essentially a translation of the Japanese term *fudoshin*. Modern hoplologists have come to view this phenomenon as a continuum ranging from steadfast mind—cool and active, in the face of fair-to-middlin' levels of danger such as one might experience in intense live-sword training in the dojo or, as Hayes puts it, "Climbing a sheer rock wall several hundred feet in height, roped to one's companions, using pitons and other climbing gear..."—to imperturbable mind. Hayes compares the imperturbable end of the continuum to, "Climbing the same rock wall without companions, without roping, and without gear, using only one's feet and hands," a situation more akin to mortal combat. One slip can mean death.

lems, devise tactics, etc. Hayes compares this to the most proficient hunters of the Paleolithic period (Hayes 1988, 9).

The key word here is "hunter," as this type of behavior is characteristic of predators. Ethologist Irenäus Eibl-Eibesfeldt contrasts this cool, calm predatory aggression (hunter behavior) to the highly aroused behavior displayed in intraspecies "affective aggression." He makes an interesting, detailed comparison of these two types of basic combative behavior, which hoplologist Hunter Armstrong has applied in analyzing actual combative systems.[13] Obviously Japanese warriors, as well as combatants from many cultures, have employed both intraspecies affective aggression—the shouting of challenges, brandishing of weapons, etc.—and interspecies predatory aggression—cool, calm stalking—on an intraspecies basis; i.e., against their human enemies.[14] Significantly, affective aggression creates a much larger energy drain on the organism than does predatory aggression. Due to practical energy requirements, any protracted mortal combat engagement requires predatory behavior—that is, mental control within the realm of imperturbable mind.

Many societies have their own terms for the ability to block the general adaptation syndrome, to function relying on predatory behavior. The German *kaltblütig*, Spanish *a sangre fria*, and French *sangfroid* are roughly equivalent to the English "cold-blooded" or "cool." In Japanese the term is *fudoshin*, literally, "immovable or imperturbable mind." This ability to block the alarm reaction and prevent precipitation of the GAS (steadfast/imperturbable mind) plays a critical role in combative behavior, for it facilitates and conditions the manifestation of not only the other two psycho-physical functions but the three body- and two action-manifested traits as well. In the grip of panic, fear, or mindless rage, the human organism would neither be able to perform with a

---

[13] See *The Biology of Peace & War* (Eibl-Eibesfeldt 1979, 32). An extrapolation of this comparison with applications to human combative behavior can be found in "The Two Faces of Combatives," (Armstrong 1994, 6-10).

[14] Armstrong defines this as "pseudo-predatory" behavior.

clear sensorium nor would—as the Japanese warrior might understand it—body, breath, and mind be able to facilitate the movement patterns necessary for combat. Thus, the steadfast/imperturbable mind is the basis from which all of the other traits operate to form a unified whole.

Cognition/Intuition

The second psycho-physical function hypothesized by Hayes is the manifest cognitive/intuitive trait; that is, the processing of sensory data by the right and left brain hemispheres in a continual flux of cognition and intuition. In a combative context, sensory data is constantly screened for signs of danger or threat. And here, depending on the intensity and immediacy of threat, the brain/mind, in a mix of cognition and intuition decides how to respond instantly, seamlessly, in order to resolve the situation. If the individual is a warrior (or some other type of combatant) with years of experience and training, he is then able to respond through the combative systems in which he has trained. Completely instantaneous action, however, requires a third function—volition.

Volition

Volition (will, initiative) is a term that covers a sometimes obscure area of human psychology. In humans this psycho-physical function has become modified by two, sometimes diametrically opposed, types of motivation, endogenous motivation—determined by our own genotypical instincts, drives, and sentiments—and exogenous motivation—determined by the values, beliefs, etc. of the various cultures in which we are raised. Current research has evidently not yet clarified whether these motivations should be classified under cognition/intuition or volition. Hoplologically, however, volition is limited to initiative within the phenomenology of combat.

In the Japanese combative context, volition is described variously as *go no sen, sen no sen,* and *sensen no sen.* All of these terms indicate a type of action taken (or, in some cases, withheld) in relation to a combative situation; i.e., the interval (in Japanese, *ma*) of space and time or even psychological distance separating opponents. In general, these terms may be translated as follows:[15]

go no sen	response action—luring an opponent into making a foolish attack so that a counterattack may be used.
sen no sen	preemptive action—using initiative to prevent the opponent's taking initiative.
sensen no sen	pre-active action—using initiative to suppress or defeat an opponent before he has a chance to contemplate an attack.

A cautionary note should be made here. While the go no sen type of volition might be viewed by an untrained observer as a vacant, waiting posture, it is not. It is, in fact, still "volitional" or "positive," and the waiting swordsman holds the initiative even though his body may be in a static posture. Then, if an enemy approaches too closely, the static posture can explosively be transformed into a lethal attack. An example of this can be found even today in the *sangakuen* strategies of the Yagyu Shinkage-ryu, a classical warrior tradition dating from the mid-1500s.[16] In these combative *kata* (prearranged movement/behavior patterns), the Yagyu Shinkage-ryu swordsman waits for an attack by the enemy swordsman. His body is in a static posture (referred to as *tai*) but it is essential that his mind be not only steadfast or imperturbable (fudoshin)

[15] Kaminoda Tsunemori, a fully licensed teacher of several Japanese martial traditions and former instructor of the Tokyo riot police (Kidotai) concurs with these definitions. For examples of their application in combative technique, see my "*Sen* and *Hyoshi*: Initiative and Rhythm in the Shindo Musoryu" (Hall 1992). Go no sen is also referred to as *machi no sen*, while sen no sen can also be *tai no tai*, and sensen no sen is also *kakari no sen* (Kaminoda 1987, 52).

[16] These strategies were originally developed during the Warring States period by Kamiizumi Ise-no-Kami Nobutsuna, founder of the Shinkage-ryu. For more detail on sangakuen see "The Yagyu Shinkageryu" (Hall 1989, 7-22).

but also filled with volition (referred to as *ken*). In other words, the assumption of a particular static posture is intended as an offering of bait; a trick used to lure the enemy into range so that he can be destroyed.[17]

These three psycho-physical functions of steadfast/imperturbable mind, cognition/intuition, and volition, act as a unified whole and facilitate manifestation of the body-bound and action-bound traits. The omnipoise, abdominal, respiratory/vocality, force/yield, and synchronous traits, in turn are expressed either through system-bound (i.e., formalized/trained) or system-free (informal/untrained/spontaneous) actions. In the case of the Japanese warrior, many years were spent training in system-bound technique. In order for the warrior to perform with a clear sensorium and properly animate system-bound technique via the above mentioned body- and action-bound traits, his volition had to be mediated by steadfast/imperturbable mind and directed by cognition/intuition. As the three psycho-physical functions were cultivated to work in a harmonious mix with the body- and action-bound traits, the acme of a warrior's development included not only physical proficiency in combative systems, but also a high level of development of the three psycho-physical functions.

MARISHITEN AND COMBATIVE SIDDHI: INVISIBILITY AND VOLITION

Having seen how these psycho-physical functions are important for the warrior, we turn now to the way they apply to the cult of Marishiten. As we have seen, the early Japanese warrior made little attempt to physically conceal himself from his enemy once he was on the battlefield. Yet reliance on Marishiten's power to make the warrior invisible and confuse his enemies is alluded to in the secret transmission scrolls of the earliest warrior traditions of the Muromachi period,[18] and

---

[17] Yagyu Nobuharu, twenty-first headmaster of the Owari line of the Yagyu Shinkage-ryu, interviews with the author, 1985-1989.

[18] For example, those of the Nen-ryu, Tenshin Shoden Katori Shinto-ryu, etc. (Hall 1990, chapter 6).

warrior devotion to Marishiten was a wide-spread phenomenon by the late Heian or early Kamakura period.

To resolve this apparent contradiction, I propose that in the case of the Japanese warrior the power of invisibility represented or granted by Marishiten was not simply a physical cloaking, but a cultivated, psychological ability. It was directly related to the manifestation of volition by a combatant and the effect of that volition on an opponent. Consequently, invisibility might indicate anything from the hiding of one's intentions (strategically or tactically), to the psychological blinding of an opponent in hand-to-hand combat. In support of this, let us take a look at a hypotheses developed by Professor Paddy Griffith, a senior lecturer at the Department of War Studies at the Royal Military Academy, Sandhurst.

Griffith, in his intensive investigation of battles from Waterloo to the recent military past discovered that, in contrast to generally accepted military theory, the victor of many of the engagements in the battles he examined was not necessarily the side that brought the most firepower to bear upon the enemy. It was, instead, the force that refused to be intimidated, that displayed a great deal of personal volition and exhibited a balance of morale and steadiness.

In one example of this, Griffith quotes I. Hamilton, a staff officer who participated in the Russo-Japanese War (1904-05):

> ...the Okasaki Brigade was crossing the open to try and storm Terayama by one supreme effort; and the only English expression which will convey an idea of their haste is that of the hunting-field, 'Hell for leather.' Bullets fell thick among those who ran for life or death across the plain, and the yellow dust of their impact on the plough rose in a cloud almost up to the men's knees. By what magic these bullets almost always struck in the vacant spaces and very rarely on the bodies of the men, I cannot explain, beyond saying that it was ever thus with the bullets of a bad shooting corps... To the best of my observation the assaulting infantry ran 600 yards without the semblance of a halt, as their leading files reached the sunken

road they dashed unhesitatingly into it, right onto the top of the crouching Russian infantry! Next second the Russians and their assailants were rushing up Terayama slopes in one confused mob, the whole mass convulsively working bayonet and bullet and clubbed rifle as they ran. The hill was carried. Bravo! Bravo!! Bravo!!! (Griffith 1990, 71)

Here, then, is a twentieth century report of an enemy practically blinded and confused (they were unable to fire effectively on the Japanese) by the power of the volition of the attacking troops. It is important to note here that Hamilton's statement concerning the marksmanship of the Russians—"...it was ever thus with the bullets of a bad shooting corps..."—does not necessarily mean that those troops were poorly trained in shooting skills. It is more that marksmanship has little to do with the fact that the troops could not hit the enemy. Jeff Cooper, a retired, combat-seasoned Marine and one of the top combat pistol authorities in the U.S. notes:

We have known several cases in which a highly qualified marksman fired a series of atrocious short-range misses, not because he couldn't shoot but because he didn't pay attention to shooting. In these cases he seems to have been thinking about the wrong things—such as the danger in which his life was placed, the anticipation of shock..." (Cooper 1985, 57)

There are many such instances recorded in the annals of warfare. Captain T. Kamozawa noted of his own experience in the Russo-Japanese War:

Looking at instances in the recent Russo-Japanese War, where the combatants fought with the very latest firearms, one is convinced that the advocates of fire effect alone are mistaken in their arguments. Victory always attended the side which, with martial spirit roused and naked sword in hand, absolutely refused to yield; which fought on resolutely to the

end, in combat after combat, and which had the grim determination of attacking and annihilating the enemy. However
great the power possessed by rifles and cannons, it is not possible by their means, and theirs alone, to either drive the enemy from his works or to repulse an enemy who bravely
advances with the intention of coming to close quarters. The
final result in each case depends absolutely on the charge with
cold steel. (Kamozawa 1911, 323)

I need not go on quoting here to make the point. It is of interest,
however, that Griffith and other authorities such as Colonel David
Hackworth in his work *About Face* (1989) comment extensively on the
importance of having the "will" or "determination" to close with the
enemy in face-to-face combat; i.e., a volition that so disturbs the enemy's composure that he becomes confused, blinded, and in many
cases becomes paralyzed[19] or flees the scene of battle. Griffith sums up:

> In view of the general reluctance of soldiers (today) to mix
> it hand to hand, it has long been recognized that the side
> which goes out and actively seeks a confrontation will enjoy a
> great psychological advantage. Provided that the enemy can
> be convinced of both your intention and your ability to reach
> him, he will in all probability run away and leave you the vic-
> tory. (1990, 180)

Marishiten and Intuition

The second psycho-physical function—cognition/intuition—is also
closely aligned with Marishiten and the Japanese warrior. As noted

---

[19] Stanley Davis notes that "well-trained, well-equipped, well-led" U.S. troops were
paralyzed on the beaches at Normandy during the D-Day invasion of 6 June 1944
(1956, 31-35). The phenomenon seems to be a modern version of the war fetters mentioned with such dread in the Icelandic sagas.

above, cognition/intuition takes place as a result of normal bicameral brain processing. However, a warrior in the midst of battle has little time to think ("normal" cognition) about what he is doing. He often must intuit the situation and, with a clear and steady mind, manifest the necessary volition through the systems he has internalized.

In the case of Japan, some warriors—martial geniuses—were able, in the midst of battle or at locations of spiritual power[20] to intuit and create highly effective strategies for combat. These strategies (*heiho* in Japanese) were not simply techniques for manipulating a weapon. They were methods requiring psycho-physical perfection; a supreme synergy of mind, breath, and body in a unified whole. This synergy would empower the warrior with the ability to defeat an enemy with what might often appear to an observer as the simplest of movements. While we may analyze these strategies through our own cognitive abilities, they were not deliberate creations arrived at through normal cognition. They were, instead, intuited in the heat of battle or as the culmination of exhaustive, protracted religious austerities. Also, these strategies are neither applied through normal, cognitive consciousness, nor are they taught through normal intellectual-pedagogical means. A master teacher passes them on to a disciple in a way that requires the student to use intuition under stressful conditions; in several martial traditions this was accomplished in front of altars dedicated to Marishiten.

Since these strategies were originally intuited in stressful situations and not intellectually constructed, they were subjectively viewed by the Japanese warrior as spiritual revelations. This is not unlike the experience of *tapas* or "sacred heat" of the Indo-Europeans. Consequently, in many secret transmission scrolls we find these intuitive leaps variously referred to as *muso* (dream-vision), *musoken* (dream-vision sword strat-

---

[20] In addition to martial shrines that were well known for this, such as those at Kashima and Katori, Buddhist locations, such as the ancient Tendai temple of Kuramadera, were also noted for martial revelations. For a more comprehensive listing of these locations see *Heihosha no Seikatsu* (Ishioka 1981, 24-39), and *Zusetsu Kobudoshi* (Watatani 1967, 142-144).

Illustration of Karanbo from a Shinkage-ryu scroll dated 1600.
Muto Masao collection.

egy), *muso shinden* (transmission of the dream-vision of the deity), *tenshin shoden* (true and correct transmission from the deity), *Kashima shinden* (a true trans mission from [the deity] of Kashima Shrine), *shinkage*,[21] *shotengu* (a correct transmission via a *tengu*),[22] and so on.

The most common of these terms is probably muso, which is apparently found much less frequently outside the martial context. Carmen Blacker, in her studies of shamanism in Japan has only encountered the term muso as a healing oracle at two temples in the Kyoto-Nara area.[23] These oracles manifest themselves in dreams while the petitioner sleeps

---

[21] The term *shinkage* (as well as several others in this list) may be written in several ways, each with a different meaning or nuance. The variant I refer to here is that combination of the characters 神 *kami* (a manifestation of spiritual power/a Shinto deity) and 影 *kage* (shadow; e.g. "influence") that is attributed to Kamiizumi Ise-no-Kami. It indicates a sacred transmission that was received under the influence of a kami.

[22] This tengu, or long-nosed goblin, is found listed as the "intermediary" between Marishiten and Nen Ami Jion, the founder of the Nen-ryu in the *Marishi-setsu Shogun Kyo*, a scroll dated ca. 1596 and attributed to Nen Ami Jion (ca. 1350-?). Higuchi family archives, Maniwa, Japan.

[23] Carmen Blacker, personal correspondence, 22 September 1989; telephone interview with the author, Tokyo, Japan, 29 September 1989.

KORYU BUJUTSU

Illustration of Marishiten as a tengu from a Hikida (Shin)kage-ryu denshō, ca. 1560. Kato collection.

in a sacred place. Muso shinden appears more than thirty times at the beginning of ryu names in the *Bugei Ryuha Daijiten* (Watatani and Yamada 1978). There are many more that contain the term.

Some of the names of the strategies transmitted in these revelations also reflect the concepts of volition, invisibility, and their divine origins. For example, the Shindo Muso-ryu (the name of which means literally Shinto Dream-Vision Tradition) includes the divinely revealed strategies *gomuso no jo* (five dream-vision staff strategies): e.g., *yamiuchi* (unperceived strike); *yumemakura* (dream revelation, literally "appearance in a dream"); *inazuma* (lightning); etc. The Shinkage-ryu's "revealed" strategies increased as the founder, Kamiizumi Nobutsuna, sought deeper insights into the art of swordsmanship. The earliest set of divine strategies were called the *tengusho* and each kata has the name of a special tengu attached to it—Karanbo, Chiraten, Konpirabo, etc. (Marishiten appears in the guise of a tengu in some Shinkage-ryu transmission scrolls, see photo above.)

A second set of revealed strategies are simply called the *okugi* ("secret principles" or "inner mysteries"). The names of these tend to vary in different branches of the Shinkage-ryu. Some of those are *gokui* (secret principle); *muniken* (sword strategy of non-duality); *shinmyoken* (ineffable sword strategy); *reikenden* (magical/miraculous sword strategy), etc.

There are many more. Often a tradition will not even reveal the names of these strategies to the uninitiated.

Again, these subtle strategies, even today, are not "taught" in an intellectual sense. Learning them requires the disciple to use intuition based on years of experience and training. This teaching approach becomes clear when viewed in light of current studies in psychology. According to current research into intuition, people possess that special ability precisely because they have mastered a relatively narrow field of endeavor (Benderly 1989, 36). Evidently the thousands of hours of effort the warrior devoted to training would have provided him with a large body of experience/knowledge that actually created a change in the way he thought and reasoned. He thus attained the ability to deal with larger "chunks" of internalized knowledge (long-term memory).

Robert Glaser, a specialist in research on intuition at the University of Pittsburgh, notes, "The performances of highly competent individuals indicate the possession of, rapid access to, and efficient utilization of an organized body of conceptual and procedural knowledge" (Benderly 1989, 36). This phenomenon of rapid access is commonly referred to as a flash of intuition. The ability to make intuitive leaps meant that a warrior or trainee had advanced past the stage of taking a plodding, analytical approach to dealing with combative situations, such as a sudden attack, and had advanced to one of instantaneous, intuitive action. Those flashes or insights experienced by the seasoned Japanese warrior—especially in the early traditions founded during the period from the fourteenth to the seventeenth centuries—were most often attributed to Marishiten (Hall 1990, chapter 6).

REVEALED STRATEGIES

In addition to cultivating intuition in the trainee, the "revealed" kata of these systems associated with Marishiten also fostered the development of steadfast/imperturbable mind and volition. By internalizing prearranged combative patterns, the practitioner was able to reduce combative stress levels by reducing the unknown. The warrior who practiced these inspired kata would not have been easily surprised in actual combative situations and the effect of his alarm reaction would have been correspondingly lower.

This is not a phenomenon restricted to Japan. The practice of prearranged combative movement/behavior patterns, aimed at cultivating steadfast/imperturbable mind, can be found in the annals of personal combat in many other cultures. A prime example is that of the Spanish fencing schools, which were founded at about the same time as some of the Japanese traditions discussed above. Egerton Castle noted in his classic *Schools and Masters of Fence:*

> Spaniards enjoyed during the whole of the sixteenth and seventeenth centuries the reputation of being very dangerous duelists, a fact which may be explained by the habit of coolness developed by those methodical notions, and the necessity of constant and careful practice for the acquisition of even a rudimentary "destreza," [dexterity and cleverness] starting from such principles. (Castle 1969, 71)[24]

In addition to this, the Spanish schools also leaned toward a psychological approach to combative practice, much in the same manner as their Japanese counterparts. Castle again noted:

> It is a remarkable fact that in Spain, the supposed birthplace of systematic swordsmanship, so little progress should have been made towards what may be called the more *practical* use of the sword. Whilst the Italians and, after their example, the French, Germans and English gradually discovered that simplification led to perfection, the Spanish masters, on the contrary, seemed to aim at making fencing a more and

---

[24] Although Castle's work has been treated as infallible by many later writers, it should be noted that there have been criticisms of his analyses. Castle considered the Spanish school's theory of "geometric complications and circular emphasis" to be inferior and felt that its deadly reputation must have been due to long practice of prearranged combative sequences; "a triumph over theory, not of theory." Tom Conroy notes that Castle's bias was due to "his linear prejudice and foil background" (Conroy 1980, 2).

more mysterious science, requiring for its practice a knowledge of geometry and natural philosophy, and whose principles were only explainable on metaphysical grounds. (Castle 1969, 67)

Castle does not go into detail on what those metaphysical grounds were. However, while the "mysticism" of Carança's Spanish system was evidently the object of extensive criticism by the Italians, French, Germans and English, the ability of the Spanish as cool, fearless combatants was well known (Wise 1971, 53).

COMBATIVE FLOW STATE

As we have already seen, this cool formidability can be explained hoplologically as an expression of the three psycho-physical functions—steadfast/imperturbable mind, cognition/intuition, and volition. This synergistic combination produces not only cool formability, it also engenders an altered state of consciousness.

M. Csikszentmihalyi of the University of Chicago has called this phenomenon the "flow state." Although his observations have been made on subjects engaged in non-combative activities, the phenomenon is similar. Csikszentmihalyi describes the state as one in which "time is distorted (and) a sense of happiness and well-being overcomes (the subject)." People in this altered state of consciousness have entered a highly *creative* psychological state, "...when things seem to go just right, when you feel alive and fully attentive to what you are doing."[25]

An interesting example can be taken from Captain Ralph Parr, a double-ace fighter pilot during the Korean War. He was involved in a six hundred m.p.h. maneuvering dog-fight that took place at an alti-

[25] Anne C. Roark quoting researcher Mihaly Csikszentmihalyi, University of Chicago. Armstrong defines the flow state as "optimum *creative* response to situations of *stress*, and based upon learned movement or behavior patterns." Correspondence from Armstrong, 7 November 1989.

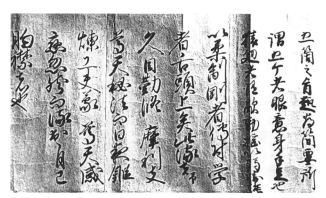

*Shinkage-ryu scroll indicating a revelation from Marishiten, dated
1565. Scroll signed by founder of Shinkage-ryu, Kamiizumi
Ise-no-Kami. Yagyu Nobuharu collection.*

tude of only about one hundred feet above tree-top level. In this engagement, he single-handedly "cornered" sixteen Migs and shot down
three. During the course of the fight, he out-maneuvered eight enemy
aircraft, eight of whom amazingly emptied their guns on him without
scoring a single hit. During the experience, he entered a combative flow
state. In the midst of battle he felt that things slowed down, giving him
time, not only to creatively outmaneuver and outshoot all his opponents, but also to notice single leaves on the trees below and count the
rivets on the nose air intake of one of his opponent's aircraft. Parr
noted:

> When you are under a tremendous amount of pressure and
> things are going very fast and there is a hell-of-a-lot at stake,
> you get so much adrenaline pumping through your system,
> your mind starts traveling at a rate of speed whereby every-
> thing seems to go into a very slow motion. You can almost
> anticipate everything. (*Combat Air Aces*, 1992)

Here with Captain Parr we see a modern example of the combative
flow state—engendered by imperturbable mind—actually facilitating
the use of intuition and taking of initiative.

Marishiten   109

In the case of the Japanese *bushi*, we find numerous accounts of warriors who entered a similar state of altered consciousness, a state of both peak-level performance and physical and psychological "non-arousal," or interdiction of alarm reaction—a flow state of high efficiency and calmness in which they were able to freely intuit effective combative strategies. For the Japanese warrior, this state was manifested through and facilitated by training in inspired prearranged movement/behavior patterns and reinforced by Marishiten-engendered confidence and morale.[26]

Watatani expressed this in the Buddhist-influenced terminology of Japanese martial culture:

> In not being caught by "winning and losing," and being flexible and free from obstructions, one can "create" technique freely. (Watatani 1967, 142)

Watatani's comment also indicates that the combative flow state borders on a sort of egolessness—a giving up of ideas of self and other, winning and losing—in order to unfetter the mind. Here we enter a new realm of combative experience.

SELFLESSNESS AND COMPASSION

If courage and success in battle were all that the Buddhist Marishiten cult offered, it would have differed little from cults of the other, often horrific, battlefield goddesses found in India: Durgâ, Kâlî, Candî, etc. However, from its earliest beginnings, the cult of Marishiten had a particularly Buddhist stamp. In becoming fully empowered by the goddess, the warrior transcends that which we normally think of as warriorship, and enters a more rarefied spiritual realm.

---

[26] See the Shinkage-ryu initiation ritual and Marishiten protection rituals of the Tenshin Shoden Katori Shinto-ryu described in chapter 6 of my *Marishiten: Buddhism and the Warrior Goddess*, 1990.

This religio-psychological connection between Buddhism and combative traditions has most often been cast in Zen terms by Japanese and Western writers. This is an understandable situation, as Zen strongly influenced the development of spiritually-oriented *budo* (martial way) systems during the Edo period. Many of those budo systems survive today and, in contrast to the more exclusive warrior traditions, have been easily accessible to writers and scholars. Consequently, those writers and scholars have often attributed important psychological concepts in this area to the influence of Zen Buddhism—i.e., fudoshin (imperturbable mind), *muga* (egolessness or selflessness), and *mushin* (freedom from discriminative thinking), etc.[27] However, while Zen thought did indeed permeate the philosophy of the classical budo, we find the concept of selflessness appearing much earlier within the cult of Marishiten, where it is associated with combative traits.

In various editions of the *Mârîcî-dhâranî-sûtra,* the goddess is described as free from fear (imperturbable mind), free from timidity (volition), and in possession of clarity and sharpness of mind (cognition/intuition). In addition, she is also free from pride, she bears no malice, and she is ungraspable because she is empty of self. Thus, she embodies selflessness.

This is important regarding combat for, as long as the warrior embodies a "grasping persona" (fear of death, concern with winning and losing, etc.; in other words, self-aggrandizement), he himself may succumb to being grasped, manipulated, and controlled. However, becoming fully empowered by the goddess, the warrior attains a state of selflessness (muga); one in which he is complete, unconcerned with winning and losing, and non-grasping. This central element of the Marishiten cult was apparent in its earliest association with combative traditions in Japan and is still important in those traditions remaining

---

[27] See, for example, D.T. Suzuki, *Zen and Japanese Culture* (1988, 61-214); E.J. Harrison, *The Fighting Spirit of Japan* (1982); E. Herrigel, *Zen in the Art of Archery* (1970); D. F. Draeger, *Classical Budo* (1973, 27-29); etc.

today. According to Otake Risuke of the Tenshin Shoden Katori Shinto-ryu, the devotee aims at attaining this ideal state of muga—egolessness—through practice of the rituals in which the warrior becomes identified with and empowered by the goddess.[28]

It is unknown how many warriors attained this ideal state, although many may have attained varying degrees of perfection approaching it. Reaching that state of selflessness—a complete interpenetration or possession by the goddess—the warrior enters a new realm of being, an awakening.

Recalling the biological basis of the combative siddhi attributed to Marishiten, we have seen how the psycho-physical functions (steadfast/imperturbable mind + cognition/intuition + volition) combine in the superior warrior in a harmonious, seamless mix in order to deal with danger/threat. Manifesting this mix via the body- and action-bound traits, the warrior was able to achieve and maintain psycho-physical dominance over an opponent.

Accordingly, the intensity of volition is dependent on the degree of danger/threat; the most important factor here is whether or not the encounter is a life-or-death situation. If safety measures are in effect—as in a training situation in which mock weapons and prearranged combative movement/behavior forms (kata) are used—the intensity of volition will be limited. However, in a real combative situation where life and death are in the balance, the intensity of volition becomes unlimited, free to adjust to whatever is required in a dangerous, free-flowing encounter. Thus, the degree to which the alarm reaction must be suppressed will move from steadfast to imperturbable mind (even steadfast mind is maladaptive for protracted combat), and intuition, volition, and their expression through combative behavior will also be unlimited.

---

[28] Interviews with Otake Risuke, Narita, Japan, 1985-1989. See also *The Deity and the Sword* (Otake 1977, vol. 3:16-18).

Thus, the actions and experience of the warrior in these two types of situations are distinct. Hayes has delineated these two modes of combat as the "lowland" and "midland" of combative experience; the lowland relates directly to the realm of limited volition (training, agonistic sports, etc.), while the midland relates directly to the realm of unlimited volition (mortal combat).[29] But, while optimum manifestation of imperturbable mind, intuition, and volition under the stresses of mortal combat make an extremely effective warrior, the cult of Marishiten offered more—and required more—of its devotees. Through the performance of Marishiten-oriented *shugyo* (austere training aimed at honing and refining his spirit and character), the warrior moved toward a realization, an interpenetration with the idealized embodiment of selflessness.

At the midland, the warrior may experience and manifest the ability to psychologically blind and befuddle enemies through superior imperturbability, intuition, volition, and inspired technique. But, both the lowland and midland of performance are bound up in the mental state of "grasping." That is, the exponent is obsessed with winning and losing, with recognition and approval, with clinging to life. In Buddhist terms we would say he is bound up in *samsâra*. This egotism is often expressed in the form of pride, machismo, or arrogance, and obviously is at odds with the ideal set forth in the *Mârîcî-dhâranî-sûtra*. Thus, mastery of the ultimate secrets of Marishiten-derived combative traditions required the warrior to engage in shugyo focused on the goddess. The aim of this shugyo was to refine the devotee into a "complete state-of-being/becoming," that is, a non-grasping state of selfless perfection. This was not viewed as an unreachable ideal; the martial texts available, such as the Marishiten-inspired *Kanjo Gokui* of the Hikida (Shin)kage-ryu, allude to this state as "the highest level of swordsman-

---

[29] Dialogues with R. Hayes and H. Armstrong, 1985-95; Hayes terms this the "Transcendent Synergy of the Manifest Adaptive Traits" (TS of the MAT) (Hayes 1994, 21-22).

ship." Realizing this state, the warrior is a *meijin* (sage) and combative behavior/ performance/experience operates at the level of the "upland."

The upland represents the idealized state in which all dualities are transcended: winning/losing, action/non-action, etc., and, as Hayes notes, "(combative) performance and outcome have such economy and elegance they can only be described as 'sublime'" (Hayes 1994, 24). Suppression of the alarm reaction is at the level of complete imperturbability, intuition facilitates anticipation of an opponent's course of action (even before he himself has thought of it), and volition operates at the level of sensen no sen, suppressing the opponent before he has a chance to contemplate an attack.

As the meijin needs no confirmation of his status and moves through the world unobserved, examples of such perfection are relegated to the realm of legend and tradition. In these stories, however, we find examples of their *myoyu* (wondrous activities). One of the most exemplary is that of Fujiwara no Yasumasa. The story describes Yasumasa, a Heian period courtier, pursued by an infamous brigand upon a wind-swept, desolate moor. (In some versions of the story the brigand is referred to as Hakamadare and the location is a deserted street of Kyoto late at night.) Yasumasa, completely relaxed and fearless, continues to play his bamboo flute and appears to ignore the brigand's approach. This so frustrates Hakamadare that he purposely makes noise in order to startle his target. Yasumasa, imperturbable, plays on. Hayes' description of the incident, as depicted in a triptych by Yoshitoshi, best describes the incident:

> ...Yasumasa, with relaxed comportment, devoid of the slightest feather of ego, pride, or hubris that the footpad's aggressive intent can snag upon, grasp, and cling to, walks on. The interval between them opens, deepens, step by step, and the footpad's initiative (volition) is proportionately sapped and drained. Yasumasa walks on. (Hayes 1994, 25)

As Yasumasa calmly walks on, his psycho-physical dominance completely confounds his opponent. Not only does Yasumasa not resort to arms, he continues to play the flute. The brigand, Hakamadare, is described as being uncannily filled with fear at the sight of Yasumasa, and unable to mount his attack.

In variants of the story, Yasumasa leads the brigand to his home and gives him clothing, admonishing him to be careful traveling alone at night as he might be set upon by bandits! In these acts of selflessness and compassion, Yasumasa represents the fulfillment of the criteria required of the devotee in quest of obtaining the empowerment of Marishiten.

The combative psycho-physical functions represented by Marishiten gave the warrior a great physical and psychological advantage in mortal combat. His body relaxed in a manner that allowed him to use energy explosively and efficiently; his mind calm, cool, and fearless, in a state of imperturbability, he entered the creative flow state where time distorted and slowed; drawing instantaneously, seamlessly, on the mass of combative knowledge and experience he had accumulated, he was able to anticipate his opponent's intent and actions, and intuit, create, and take the initiative in executing the most effective course of action or non-action. Having honed his character through arduous training and unification with the goddess through shugyo, he became selfless. Being empty of self, he neither grasped nor could he be grasped. Just like Marishiten,

> No one can see him, no one can know him, no one can seize him, no one can harm him, no one can deceive him, no one can fetter him, no one can cloud his mind, and he does not bear malice.

The exhilaration of the combative flow state can be addicting. This is apparent across cultures and time. The intensity of the altered consciousness experienced in mortal combat is, for many, the most meaningful experience in their lives. In his *Journal of a Plague Year*, a U.S. Navy doctor stationed in Vietnam recounted the following conversation with a young Marine who had volunteered for a second tour in the war zone:

"I don't really know why I came back, Doc… I just did… I tried to go back to school but nothing seemed relevant or interesting… Those kids in class were so… sincere and got all worked up over such unimportant things… You know, Doc, nothing seemed important. I mean like nothing. My job, my paycheck, school, my friends. Nothing. They were all a drag."

"So?" asked Dr. Parrish.

"So, here, everything is important. I mean it's important as hell if you wear your helmet or not. An untied boot lace may cost you your life. It's important where you sleep, when you sleep, and who's next to you and who's awake while you sleep… It's important how and where I walk, when and how much I eat. My job here is important as hell… Back home nothing I did was important and here every… little thing I do is important as hell!" (Parrish 1972, 251-253)

The young Marine is not alone. Many are those who, having undergone the combative flow state, have become career combatants or engage in dangerous sports, seeking to once again undergo that meaningful experience. This passion is as much a part of our human nature as any other desire. And, from the Buddhist point of view, like other passions it binds us into an endless chain of cause and effect, egotistical craving, and suffering. The cult of Marishiten is a prime example of the way in which Tantric Buddhist *upâya* (compassionate, skillful means) was used to bring warriors and other combatants away from suffering and into the Buddhist path, not by rejection of the most meaningful experience in their lives, but by ultimately redirecting that very experience toward selflessness and compassion.

References

Combat Air Aces. 1992. *The Challenge Program.* The Discovery Channel.

Armstrong, H.B. 1994. The Two Faces of Combatives. *Hoplos* 7, no. 3:6-10.

Benderly, B.L. 1989. Everyday Intuition: Experience, Recognition, Insight. *Psychology Today.* September.

Castle, E. 1969. *Schools and Masters of Fence.* York, PA: G. Shumway.

Conroy, T. 1980. Errors and Oversights in Castle's *Schools and Masters of Fence,* Part 1. *Hoplos* 2, no. 3.

Cooper, J. 1985. The Combat Mind Set. *American Handgunner.* July/August.

Davidson, H.R.E. 1988. *Myths and Symbols in Pagan Europe: Early Scandinavian and Celtic Religions.* Syracuse: Syracuse University Press.

Davis, S.W. 1956. Stress in Combat. *Scientific American* 194, no. 3.

Draeger, D.F. 1973. *Classical Budo.* The Martial Arts and Ways of Japan, 2. New York & Tokyo: Weatherhill.

Draeger, D.F., and R.W. Smith. 1969. *Asian Fighting Arts.* Tokyo: Kodansha.

Eibl-Eibesfeldt, I. 1979. *The Biology of Peace & War.* New York: The Viking Press.

Griffith, P. 1990. *Forward into Battle: Fighting Tactics From Waterloo to the Near Future.* 2nd ed. Wiltshire: Crowood Press.

Hackworth, D.H., and J. Sherman. 1989. *About Face : the Odyssey of an American Warrior.* New York: Simon and Schuster.

Hall, D.A. 1990. *Marishiten: Buddhism and the Warrior Goddess*. Ann Arbor: University Microfilms.

———. 1992. Sen and Hyoshi. *IJF Newsletter*: 2-3.

———. 1989. The Yagyu Shinkageryu: Part 2. *Hoplos* 6, no. 4:7-22.

Hamilton, L. 1989. Fight, Flight or Freeze: Implications of the Passive Fear Response for Anxiety and Depression. *Phobia Practice and Research Journal* 2, no. 1:17-27.

Harrison, E.J. 1982. *The Fighting Spirit of Japan*. Woodstock, New York: Overlook Press.

Hayes, R. 10 October 1989. Letter to David A. Hall.

———. 1988. Hoplology Theoretics, an Overview. Part 4: The Innate/Manifest. *Hoplos* 6, no. 3:7-12.

———. 1994. Hoplology Theoretics, an Overview. Part 8. *Hoplos* 7, no. 3.

Hayes, R., and D.F. Draeger, *Hoplology Theoretics—Vol. I: Conceptual Tools for the Hoplologist*. 1984. ed. M.P. Belzer. Seattle: Privately published.

Herrigel, E. 1970. *Zen in the Art of Archery*. New York: Pantheon Books.

Ishioka, H. 1981. *Heihosha no Seikatsu* (The Strategist's Life). Tokyo: Yuuzankaku Shuppan.

Ishioka, H., and S. Arima. 1967. *Shoryu Heiho (Part 1)* (Martial Strategies of Various Traditions). Nippon Heiho Zenshu, 6. Tokyo.

Kaminoda, T. 1987. *Isshin-ryu Kusarigamajutsu.* Tokyo: T. Kaminoda.

Kamozawa, C.T. 1911. The Value of the *"Arme Blanche,"* From Actual Instances in the Russo-Japanese Campaign. *The Cavalry Journal* 6.

Kitagawa, H., and B.T. Tsuchida, trans. 1975. *The Tale of the Heike.* Tokyo: University of Tokyo Press.

Morris, D. 1967. *The Naked Ape.* London: Jonathan Cape.

Otake, R. 1977. *The Deity and the Sword: Katori Shinto Ryu.* Tokyo: Minato Research.

Parrish, J.A. 1972. *Journal of a Plague Year: 12, 20 & 5, A Doctor's Year in Vietnam.* New York: Dutton.

Sasama, Y. 1987. *Nippon Katchu Daikan* (The Encyclopedia of Japanese Armor). Tokyo: Satsuki Shoubou.

Selye, H. 1974. *Stress Without Distress.* Philadelphia: Lippincott.

Suzuki, D.T. 1988. *Zen and Japanese Culture.* Tokyo: C. E. Tuttle.

Watatani, K. 1967. *Zusetsu Kobudoshi.* (An Illustrated History of the Classical Martial Arts). Tokyo: Seiyabou.

Watatani, K. and Yamada, T. 1978. *Bugei Ryuha Daijiten* (Dictionary of Japanese Martial Art Traditions). Tokyo: Tokyo Kopii Shuppanbu.

Wise, A. 1971. *The Art and History of Personal Combat.* Greenwich, Conn: New York Graphic Society.

Yamashita, H., ed. 1972. *Taiheiki.* Shincho Nippon Koten Shusei. Tokyo: Shinchousha.

Meik Skoss has lived and trained in Japan since 1973 and is a member of the Shinto Muso-ryu, Toda-ha Buko-ryu, Tendo-ryu, and Yagyu Shinkage-ryu. He also practices several modern arts. (Portions of the following originally appeared in "Jujutsu and Taijutsu," Aikido Journal, 1995.)

Tenjin Shinyo-ryu Jujutsu

Meik Skoss

Introduction: The Nature of Japanese Jujutsu

Japanese unarmed grappling arts have been around for a very long time, supposedly since the mythological creation of the country by the gods.[1] The first references to such unarmed combat arts or systems can be found in the earliest so-called historical records of Japan, the *Kojiki* (Record of Ancient Matters) and the *Nihon Shoki* (Chronicles of Japan), both of which relate the establishment of the Imperial family as rulers of the nation. Other glimpses of close combat can be found in the older records and pictures depicting *sumai* (or *sumo*) *no sechie*, a rite of the Imperial Court in Nara and Kyoto performed for purposes of divination and to help ensure a bountiful harvest. These types of unarmed combat were systematized during the Muromachi period (1333-1568), according to the historical records and the *densho* (transmission scrolls) of the various *ryuha* (martial traditions, "schools").

Although the classical grappling arts are most commonly referred to today under the general rubric of *jujutsu*, there were, in fact, many different names for these types of techniques and tactics, varying from *ryu* to ryu. *Hade, hakuda, jujutsu, kempo* (Sekiguchi-ryu, Araki-ryu, Seigo-ryu), *koppo, kogusoku, koshi no mawari* (Takenouchi-ryu and Yagyu Shingan-ryu), *kowami, kumiuchi, shubaku, tode, torite, yawara* (Tatsumi-ryu and Shosho-ryu), *yawaragi* (Tenshin Shoden Katori Shinto-ryu), and *yoroi kumiuchi* (Yagyu Shingan-ryu) are a few of the

---

[1] The information in the introduction on the nature of Japanese jujutsu and the development of unarmed close combat systems is taken primarily from the *Nihon Kobudo Sokan* (1988, 13-32), *Nihon Budo Ryuso-den* (Kawauchi 1954, iii-iv), and *Kakutogi no Rekishi* (Fujiwara 1990, 1-5, 431-475).

Toshihiro Kubota, menkyo kaiden, performing
at the Meiji Shrine demonstration, 1996.

terms that have been used over the years. In some traditions, such as
the Takenouchi-ryu and Yagyu Shingan-ryu, more than one term was
used to refer to distinct portions of their curricula, and in fact, each of
these words denotes systems with different content or slightly varied
technical characteristics.

These close combat methods were an important, if secondary, part of
the martial systems developed by warriors for use on both the battlefield and in more peaceful situations. They can generally be characterized as either Sengoku jidai (Warring States period, 1467-1568) *katchu
bujutsu* (fighting with weapons or grappling while clad in armor), or
Edo jidai (Edo period, 1600-1868) *suhada bujutsu* (fighting, with or
without weapons, while dressed in the everyday street clothing of the
period, the kimono and *hakama*). The latter-day suhada bujutsu were

more warrior systems of self-defense than they were arts oriented toward battlefield combat.

Yoroi kumiuchi, a katchu bujutsu, may be defined, based on the curricula of many of the classical Japanese systems, as unarmed methods of battlefield combat for dealing with an enemy who was armed, together with methods of using minor weapons such as the *jutte* (truncheon), *tanto* (knife), *yoroidoshi* (armor-piercing dagger), or *kabutowari* (helmet-splitter) to defeat both armed or unarmed opponents. Yoroi kumiuchi also included tactics for infighting with the warrior's major weapons: the *ken* or *tachi* (sword), *yari* (spear), *naginata* (glaive), and *bo* (staff).

Jujutsu and similar grappling arts, which are properly classified as suhada bujutsu, are close combat systems used to defeat or control an enemy or opponent in a peacetime situation, who may or may not be armed, and who is almost never in armor. The basic methods of attack and control in such arts include: hitting, striking, thrusting, punching, kicking, throwing, pinning or immobilizing, strangling or choking, joint-locking, tying up the opponent with different types of restraining cords, and the occasional use of weapons such as the jutte, *tessen,* and *kodachi.* Great pains were also taken by the *bushi*, or classical warriors, to develop effective methods of defense against all manner of armed and unarmed attacks, and they practiced parrying or blocking strikes, thrusts and kicks, receiving throws or joint-locking techniques by learning how to fall safely and knowing how to "blend" to neutralize the technique's effect, effecting a release from an enemy's grasp, and changing or shifting position to evade or neutralize an enemy's attack.

THE DEVELOPMENT OF UNARMED AND CLOSE COMBAT SYSTEMS

Compared with the empty-handed fighting arts of neighboring China and Korea, the Japanese systems place more emphasis on joint-locking, throwing, immobilizing or pinning, and strangling techniques. In most classical Japanese martial traditions, unarmed *atemiwaza* (techniques for assaulting the vital points of the human body) are of secondary importance, but in the many Chinese arts subsumed under *ch'uan-fa* (J. *kempo*) more importance is placed on punching, striking, and kicking with the body's natural weapons. It is generally believed that hakuda, kempo, and shubaku display a greater degree of Chinese influence in their particular stress on atemiwaza, while systems derived from more purely Japanese sources show no special preferences for such techniques but will use them as and when appropriate.

There are several reasons why Japanese unarmed fighting arts developed in this way. First, the context in which they evolved, the battlefield of the Sengoku jidai helped to shape them. Combat was then typically a matter of large-scale battlefield engagements. Bushi, dressed in armor and armed with powerful weapons, fought all over the place of battle, in what amounted to a melee situation, on various types of terrain. These were not the sort of conditions where striking an enemy with fists or feet would be terribly effective. Further, the usual close-quarters tactics of the day called for closing with an enemy, throwing him down, and then taking his head.

Another reason for this lesser emphasis on atemiwaza in Japanese systems created for use on the battlefield is the fact that, even if one were able to penetrate an enemy's armor or protective equipment, it would be exceedingly difficult to defeat a trained fighter with one blow by killing or incapacitating him; failure is more likely than success in such a circumstance. If the attempt fails, the enemy will use the weapon he is carrying to cut you down. The most important thing then, when one is grappling on the battlefield, is to prevent the enemy from using his weapon. If possible, you must be able to control his hands to prevent him from bringing his weapon to bear. If he does manage to do so, then you must be able to stop him from using it against you. On the other hand, if you are the one with the weapon, you must be able to free yourself from the enemy's grasp, open sufficient distance to move freely, then apply an effective counterattack. In battlefield combat, warriors are both mentally and physically prepared for life-and-death conflict and this factor must also be taken into account.

In peacetime, however, there is less likelihood of actual combat and a greater chance that one will be involved in a situation of self-defense. There may very well be an element of surprise involved, when one has been suddenly, unexpectedly attacked. Furthermore, it would be very unusual for the attacker to be wearing heavy armor. In this scenario, with both of the combatants dressed in everyday clothing, the use of atemiwaza becomes a highly effective element in subduing an opponent. It was this aspect of close combat in the peacetime society of the Tokugawa shogunate that led to the development of what we now usually refer to as jujutsu.

A warrior would generally resort to his sword when he was threatened, but there were certain situations in which he was not permitted to use it. In fact, there were times when using one's weapons was either difficult or impossible. One instance was in a lord's castle. The events recounted in *Chushingura* (The Story of the Forty-seven Ronin), where Lord Asano draws his short sword within Edo Castle and unsuccessfully attempts to cut down Lord Kira for having insulted him are a case in point. This was an offense punishable by death. Asano's life and domain were therefore forfeit; this, in turn, led to the famous vendetta. Had he been more skillful in close-quarters fighting, Asano's warriors could, perhaps, have avoided all of that trouble.

Another typical use of unarmed techniques by warriors was when a high-ranking warrior was attacked by one of lower status. In such a case, even if a low-ranked warrior, an *ashigaru* (foot soldier, the lowest level of bushi) for example, were to attack, say, a general, with a drawn sword, it would have been unseemly for the higher officer to use a weapon against such a common person. A further instance was when the *yoriki* and *doshin,* Tokugawa law enforcement officials, had to arrest a higher-ranking warrior for an infraction of the law. They needed to be able to do so without cutting him down, except under the most extreme circumstances. Warriors thus needed to be able to control and subdue their opponents in a manner befitting their, or their opponent's, social status.

The Development of the Tenjin Shinyo-ryu

Tenjin Shinyo-ryu is very typical of the koryu jujutsu schools extant in Japan today. It is particularly noted for its very effective grappling techniques (pinning, joint-locking and choking or strangling), its comprehensive use of techniques for assaulting an opponent's vital or anatomical weak points, and its methods of resuscitation, as well as the

Tenjin Shinyo-ryu Jujutsu

usual throws, in its practice. Jigoro Kano drew on these techniques in his creation of the more modern art of Kodokan judo. Tenjin Shinyo-ryu, in turn, was based on the techniques of two other classical jujutsu traditions, the Yoshin-ryu and Shin no Shinto-ryu.[2]

The Yoshin-ryu was founded by Akiyama Shirobei Yoshitoki, a doctor who lived in Nagasaki during the latter part of the seventeenth century and who specialized in treating children. During the time Akiyama was living in China to further his medical education, he was able to learn three techniques for unarmed combat from a local man. These Chinese methods were rather different from Japanese jujutsu of the time in that they relied almost exclusively on punching and kicking. In addition to learning these fighting techniques, Yoshitoki also studied some twenty-eight methods of resuscitation and treating injuries before he returned to Japan. Unfortunately, no one wanted to study with him because he had only these three unarmed, jujutsu-like combat techniques, and potential students were looking for more comprehensive systems. In frustration he retreated to the Dazaifu Tenmangu Shrine in Chikuzen (present-day Fukuoka) for one hundred days, and after a period of meditation and solo training, he devised a further three hundred techniques. It was while he was praying at the shrine that he saw how a willow tree's branches bent under a heavy load of snow and then shed the load without breaking. This gave him a profound insight into the importance of flexibility of mind, body, and technique and he named his school Yoshin-ryu (Spirit of the Willow School/Style) in light of this inspiration.

[2] The material on the history, content of the Tenjin Shinyo-ryu curriculum, technical characteristics, and current activities comes from articles by Kubota Toshihiro in *Nihon Densho Bugei Ryuha* (Miyazaki 1994, 26-29), *Nihon Kobudo Sokan* (1988, 41), program notes from classical martial arts demonstrations given by the Nihon Kobudo Shinkokai in 1980 and 1985, other classical martial arts demonstrations at the Nippon Budokan, 1978-1997, and personal communications with Kubota and other exponents of the ryu, 1978-1997.

Toshishiro Kubota demonstrating at Meiji Shrine demonstration, 1996.

Shin no Shinto-ryu was the creation of Yamamoto Tamizaemon Hidehaya, a guard at Osaka Castle. He had studied Yoshin-ryu jujutsu, attaining quite a high degree of skill, before going on to found his own system. He divided his new system into three graded levels, *shodan, chudan,* and *jodan* (basic, intermediate, and advanced), and also re-duced the overall number of techniques to a total of sixty-eight.

Iso Mataemon Masatari, the founder of Tenjin Shinyo-ryu, studied both of these traditions. He was born as Okamoto Hachiroji in 1787 in Ise Matsuzaka (in present-day Mie Prefecture), to a low-ranking warrior family of the Kishu domain. He died in 1863, aged 76, in Edo (present-day Tokyo).

At the age of fifteen he traveled to Kyoto and began to train under Hitotsuyanagi Oribe, a master teacher of Yoshin-ryu jujutsu, until the latter's death some seven years later. Okamoto then entered the dojo of Homma Jouemon, a well-known teacher of the Shin no Shinto-ryu who had studied with Yamamoto, the founder of the tradition. He studied with Homma for six years before receiving certification of his mastery of the principles and techniques of the style. He then began to travel throughout Japan, visiting and training with jujutsu instructors of the different feudal domains, to further improve his understanding and skills. Okamoto engaged in a series of *shiai* (training matches) with jujutsu exponents in the places he visited and it is said that he was never defeated in these bouts.

During his travels, Okamoto stopped in Kusatsu (in present-day Shiga Prefecture) for three years to teach jujutsu. On one occasion, in the company of one of his students, Nishimura Tokinosuke, he came to the aid of a man under attack, and became embroiled in a fight with more than one hundred ruffians. Okamoto's many years of training in the martial arts enabled him to chase away all of the assailants and it was at this point that he first came to truly understand the efficacy of the sophisticated use of atemiwaza.

Prior to this time, the use of atemiwaza in yoroi kumiuchi was a minor, specialized skill, but it seems not to have been thoroughly studied for use in peacetime situations. Okamoto understood that it was virtually impossible to overcome multiple opponents in a life-and-death struggle and it was with the aim of helping teach people to protect themselves that he devoted himself to a concentrated study of *shin no ate* (the use of one's natural weapons [hands, arms, and feet] for assaulting anatomical weak points of the body). He came to a profound understanding of atemiwaza after several more years of study. He then incorporated this knowledge of *atemi* into his own system of jujutsu, along with many other techniques for choking or strangling, joint-locking, and throwing an opponent. He also continued to carefully examine the principles of flexibility and balance in close combat, and learned how to avoid being defeated by the power of his opponent through skillful use of *kuzushi* (off-balancing of the opponent) by not resisting his opponent unnecessarily, and taking advantage of momentary lapses in his opponent's attention and openings in his defenses, then responding in an appropriate manner to the opponent's attack in many different circumstances.

Although the exact date of its founding is unknown, Okamoto probably began to call his new style Tenjin Shinyo-ryu sometime shortly after 1800. The characters *ten* (天) and *jin* (神) refer to what he felt was the divine quality of the revelation he had gained into the nature of unarmed combat. He had a realization similar to that of Akiyama when he saw a willow tree swaying in a high wind without breaking and realized the importance of physical and mental flexibility in close combat. The second word in the name of the school was derived by taking the characters *shin* (真) and *yo* (楊) from the names of the *Shin* no Shinto-ryu and the *Yo*shin-ryu, Iso's way of honoring the two schools he had studied.

Yo refers to a flexible type of willow tree, the *kawa yanagi*. It does not "resist," but rather bends under a heavy load of snow or against a strong wind, without breaking. The essence of the Yoshin-ryu is this flexible approach to combat, where the exponent deflects an attack and uses the opponent's power and movement to one's own advantage. The ability to respond to an enemy's attack as it occurs, avoiding being off-balanced, even momentarily, was also an essential principle. "Shin" means truth, genuineness, or reality. In this case, the word probably refers to an understanding of these essential principles of combat.

Before assuming the name Iso, Okamoto briefly called himself Kuriyama Mataemon. A change in his personal circumstances enabled him to become a direct vassal of the Tokugawa shogunate and he entered the Iso family as its successor. He then took a name that better fit his new status, Iso Mataemon Ryukansai Minamoto (no) Masatari.[3]

Iso opened a dojo in Otamagaike, in what is now the Kanda area of Tokyo. Again, the date he did this is not clearly known. Some time after that, he received an appointment as a jujutsu instructor to the Kobusho, the martial arts training school for the Tokugawa shogunate. He was a most effective teacher and classes at both his own dojo and the Kobusho proved to be quite popular. He taught more than five thousand students in the years between the Kanei and Bunku eras (1848-1864) and it is believed that Tenjin Shinyo-ryu was the most widely practiced system of jujutsu of the time.

Iso's training hall was located just across the street from the Gembukan, the kenjutsu dojo of the famous Hokushin Itto-ryu swordsman, Chiba Shusaku. The two maintained a warm relationship and many of their students trained at both schools, forming friendships that lasted over the years. They also taught each other something of their respective arts. One example of this was when Iso taught Chiba a technique called *sukuiashi* (foot scoop). This was used to sweep an opponent's foot and throw him down when kenjutsu trainees were locked together with swords crossed at the guards, each man pushing at the other to force an opening, a position known as *tsubazeriai*. In turn, Chiba likely imparted some of his knowledge of swordsmanship to the Tenjin Shinyo-ryu in some of the techniques where the jujutsu exponent must deal with an opponent who is armed with a long or short sword.

After the Meiji Restoration of 1868, instructors of jujutsu, as well as those of the other classical martial arts, fell on hard times. Most Japanese came to ignore or spurn their older culture and traditional arts in favor of the newer, more "modern" Western ways in their rush to modernize the country's industry and society.

---

[3] The way Iso changed names over the course of his life was not at all unusual for people of the Edo period. Ryukansai is a *go*, a sort of pseudonym sometimes assumed by important people to indicate some significant skills or as a sign of their social position.

This was the prevailing situation when the founder of Kodokan judo, Jigoro Kano, began to study Tenjin Shinyo-ryu jujutsu with Fukuda Hachinosuke in 1877. Kano continued his training with the third-generation headmaster of the ryu, Iso Mataemon Masatomo, when Fukuda died two years later. Finally, after

Tenjin Shinyo-ryu students demonstrating a masutemi technique, Riverside Sports Center, 1995.

training hard for a period of several more years, he mastered the *okugi* or *ogi* (secret teachings or principles) of the art: *junan na shintai* (keeping the body flexible, so one doesn't use excess, or unnecessary strength); *shintai no chushin wo tadasu* (maintaining one's body in a balanced, correct posture); and *aite wo kuzusu* (unbalancing one's opponent).

Kano continued to elaborate and to develop his understanding and application of these concepts over the years, and espoused them as both a martial artist and an educator. Eventually, in 1922, he established the guiding principles of judo as *seiryoku zenyo* (maximum efficient use of energy) and *jita kyoei* (mutual benefit and welfare). In addition, he introduced a number of jujutsu techniques into judo, many of them from the Tenjin Shinyo-ryu, after he had modified them to improve the safety for its practitioners. This was necessary because of the inherently dangerous nature of jujutsu techniques, which prevented them from being used in freestyle training. Tenjin Shinyo-ryu techniques included in judo are: *koshinage* (hip throw), *seoinage* (shoulder throw), *ashibarai* (foot sweep), *haraigoshi* (sweeping hip throw), *sukuiashi* (foot scoop), *kuchikitaoshi* (one-hand drop), *osotogari* (major outer reaping throw), *sumigaeshi* (corner throw), and various *masutemi* (rear sacrifice) and *yokosutemi* (side sacrifice) throws, as well as many of the immobilization, joint locks, and strangling techniques.

Curriculum section	Name Translation	Number
te hodoki	introductory or rudimentary techniques	12 techniques
shodan idori	basic seated techniques	10 techniques
shodan tachiai	basic standing techniques	10 techniques
chudan idori	intermediate seated techniques	14 techniques
chudan tachiai	intermediate standing techniques	14 techniques
nagesute	lit., to discard or throw away	20 techniques
shiai ura	lit., the inside or reverse of bout[s] or contest[s]	24 techniques
gokui jodan tachiai	highest, ultimate, most secret, advanced standing techniques	10 techniques
gokui jodan idori	highest, ultimate, most secret, advanced seated techniques	10 techniques

The Tenjin Shinyo-ryu is divided into nine sets of techniques,
plus three other sections that are not considered part of the main curriculum.

THE STRUCTURE OF TENJIN SHINYO-RYU JUJUTSU

There are one hundred twenty-four techniques in the Tenjin Shinyo-ryu jujutsu curriculum, five *kuden* (oral teachings), *randori-ho* (free-fighting methods), and a number of *kappo* (resuscitation methods or techniques). According to Watatani Kiyoshi and Yamada Tadashi (1978, 601-602), the curriculum also included kenjutsu and *hojojutsu* (binding art, using a tying cord to restrain prisoners), but I have seen no evidence of this in examining any of the Tenjin Shinyo-ryu densho or in talking to its teachers and senior exponents.

Students receive licenses denoting their degree of proficiency, rather than "ranks" as such, when they have trained for a sufficient period of time and show an appropriate level of skill. It should be noted here that, when I discuss the licenses awarded in Tenjin Shinyo-ryu, I am referring to those given by Mr. Kubota Toshihiro, the president of the Tenyokai. This is a group of people dedicated to the practice of Kodokan judo and Tenjin Shinyo-ryu jujutsu. Kubota Sensei is a highly qualified teacher of both Kodokan judo (graded *nanadan,* seventh-degree) and the Sakamoto Fusataro line of Tenjin Shinyo-ryu, in which he

KORYU BUJUTSU

holds a *menkyo kaiden* (license of complete transmission) and the position of *shihanke* (master teacher).

The curriculum is taught in a series of nine sets (see chart p. 132).

The twelve techniques in *te hodoki* and the ten *kata* in each of the *shodan idori* and *tachiai* sets involve a series of defenses, releases and throws from being grabbed, as well as other attacks, including strikes, thrusts, and throws. The major emphasis at this stage of training is the development of correct technique and the avoidance of undue use of strength. These kata form the basis for more advanced training methods and techniques and they are used to establish the fundamental movement and breathing patterns.

These three sets comprise the curriculum of the *shoden menjo* (basic, or primary, license), which is given as a *kirigami menjo,* a simple piece of folded Japanese paper rather than as a scroll. As a rule of thumb, one would receive this after about two years of regular training.

The *chudan idori* and *tachiai* kata, which are comprised of fourteen techniques each, are somewhat more combative or realistic in nature, but great stress continues to be placed on correct movement and refining technique. After a trainee has gained proficiency in the chudan idori and chudan tachiai techniques, generally after five or so years of regular practice, he may be awarded a *chuden,* the intermediate level license. This license is also a kirigami menjo.

The *nagesute* series is very combative in nature and techniques in this section of the curriculum are very realistic, useful in situations when one is facing multiple opponents. After ten years or so, if the student has made sufficient technical progress, he may be presented a *mokuroku* (lit., a catalog or list). The mokuroku is the first of the Tenjin Shinyo-ryu licenses that is given in the form of a *makimono* (traditional scroll), and includes a list of techniques and the lineage of the ryu, along with the date of issue and the seals used for authenticating the license.

The techniques of the *shiai ura* kata are rather difficult to characterize. Shiai means bout or match. The implication here is that these techniques are not merely for training (and certainly not for sporting competition), but for actual combat. *Ura* means, in the literal sense, reverse, opposite or inside. Shiai ura techniques are comprised, for the

Tenjin Shinyo-ryu Jujutsu   133

most part, of counter techniques, *kaeshiwaza,* methods to reverse or escape from techniques the opponent is trying to apply to one. Several of these techniques, though, are preemptive in nature, *sensen no sen* in Japanese. In these techniques the Tenjin Shinyo-ryu exponent forestalls the opponent's attack by "reading" his intention, applying the appropriate technique to counter his movements as, or even before,

Kubota Toshihiro perofrming a disarming technique against a kodachi, Meiji Srhine, 1996.

they occur. This sort of training is very common in the classical martial arts since it is what a warrior needed to prepare for actual combat.

The *gokui jodan tachiai* and *idori* sections of the curriculum are a little different from those of the basic and intermediate levels inasmuch as the sequence of studying the seated and standing techniques is reversed. These techniques require the exponent to demonstrate a fine-tuned ability to discriminate the opponent's timing and intent, and sophis-

Koryu Bujutsu

ticated methods of entering inside his defenses. When the trainee has mastered the gokui jodan tachiai waza to a sufficient degree, along with those of the shiai ura section, he may be given a *menkyo* (license), also a scroll. This degree of accomplishment, in the classical martial arts, is generally considered the first level at which an exponent is considered to be quite competent in the principles, techniques, and related technical matters pertaining to the art. Today, the time required to reach this level is usually about fifteen years of regular practice, assuming one has been able to study directly with a *shihan*, or master teacher.

Additionally, advanced trainees learn the kappo, randori-ho, and the five teachings of the kuden. These teachings constitute the highest level of instruction, the menkyo kaiden, which represents the complete, or total, transmission of the school's techniques and principles. This is the first scroll that includes a preface of written teachings or discussions, along with the list of techniques, the lineage, and the date of the license being awarded.

The Tenjin Shinyo-ryu kuden form the basis of Kodokan judo's *itsutsu no kata* (five forms), a series of five unnamed techniques that are very abstract in appearance and are said to represent the theoretical basis of Kodokan judo's throwing techniques. The Tenjin Shinyo-ryu kuden, though, have evocative names that conjure up the feeling or image of the principle involved. If one sees these movement sequences with no prior knowledge of what they represent, they may seem ineffective and silly, without any definite purpose. It is only after one has trained for a long period of time, and acquired sufficient skill in the techniques, that it becomes possible to understand and internalize what the movements "mean" in a practical sense. They are, in a very real sense, the essence of the Tenjin Shinyo-ryu's approach to unarmed combat.

CHARACTERISTICS OF TENJIN SHINYO-RYU JUJUTSU

All the kata in Tenjin Shinyo-ryu start with a distinctive utterance by both the *torimi* (the person who "takes" the technique, the person who applies the technique) and the *ukemi* (person who "receives" the technique, the person to whom the technique is applied). It is a forceful, fairly high-pitched "yip" that occurs with a dynamic compression of air in the exponent's abdomen. This has a two-fold purpose: first, it is torimi's signal that he is ready for the technique to begin, along with ukemi's signal he is starting the technique; secondly, it allows for *ki wo mitasu,* a sort of combined physiological and psychological preparation by torimi and ukemi for this imminent "combat"—they "fill themselves with *ki.*"

One of the more important teachings in Tenjin Shinyo-ryu is *"Shikiryoku goitsu fuji no myo:* [There is an] incomparable, exquisite quality when the willpower, spirit, and strength are combined and act together." The school emphasizes development and proper use of ki, or vital energy, in its training. One method for this is, as explained above, by concentrating one's ki in the lower abdomen at the beginning of a kata. Great care is also taken in learning how to read the strength of the opponent's intent and his purpose by observing him during the course of the technique. One does not approach or attack the opponent aimlessly, nor does one apply a technique mechanically, on the assumption that it will automatically be effective. This careful observation and meticulous attention to detail is an essential quality of warrior training.

Another facet of Tenjin Shinyo-ryu that shows a classical character is its use of initiative, *sen* in Japanese. The *tori* (another way to say torimi) does not always perform the techniques in what might be considered a "defensive" manner. In many kata, he attacks the *uke* (ukemi), initiating the movement in accordance with the principle of *kobo itchi,* attack and defense are "one," forming a coherent unity of action and response in combat. In other words, torimi might appear to initiate the conflict, but he does so without an offensive spirit, insofar as he is merely responding to the hostile intent he has perceived in his opponent.

Tori and uke will often begin a kata while they are several meters apart. Depending on the form, one or the other of them will close to a position in front of, behind, or to the side of his opponent, utter the beginning cry, and begin the technique. This closing of the interval, and its timing, are an important part of the training.

Almost all techniques include atemiwaza, though they are not always obvious to a casual observer. Additionally, many Tenjin Shinyo-ryu

Kubota Toshihiro performing a throwing technique,
Meiji Shrine, 1996.

techniques involve pressure being applied to the opponent's *kyusho* (the vital or anatomical weak points of the human body), to cause pain and obtain an advantage or the opportunity to press a further attack.

Tenjin Shinyo-ryu uses several *kamae* (combative engagement stances) in its training. Seated kamae include *heiza,* the seated posture usually referred to as *seiza; hira no kamae,* a half-kneeling position with one leg tucked under the body, flat on the floor, and the other up on the foot, at a right angle, close to the body; and *hira no ichimonji,* which is similar to hira no kamae, but with the raised leg extended further out—this latter is probably the basis for the *kyoshi no kamae* or high kneeling engagement posture of judo's *katame no kata.* The standing techniques use two kamae: *chokuritsu,* straight standing, identical to the judo *shizentai* or natural body stance, and a standing variant of ichimonji which is similar to, and the basis for, the defensive stance of judo known as *jigotai.*

The hira and ichimonji no kamae are distinctive in that the center of gravity is somewhat lowered and the hands are held close together, fingertips and thumbs pointing toward one another, in front of the lower abdomen. This is not to protect the groin from a punch or kick, as some people have theorized, but to assist in developing the strong concentration of ki before and after a technique that is characteristic of the Tenjin Shinyo-ryu.

<small>Training Wear and Equipment</small>
Training is usually conducted in the standard *judogi* (judo training uniforms), consisting of an *uwagi* or jacket, *zubon* or trousers, and *obi,* belt. For demonstration purposes, exponents will wear a *hakama,* a divided, skirt-like pair of culottes, worn over kimono, and a cloth headband, called a *teppi.* This originally had a thin iron plate sewn inside the folds of cloth to serve as a form of minimal protection against attacks to the head.

During the Tokugawa period, people trained in a lightweight training jacket and hakama, which was part of the everyday dress for warriors. A hakama is not very convenient to wear while training in grappling, though, as it is easy for one's legs to become entangled and there is some danger of injury. It thus became common during the Meiji period for trainees to wear a jacket and a pair of short trousers (which look like a pair of Bermuda shorts in several illustrations of the period I have seen), with the jacket secured by a cotton sash. This uniform, after modification, became the model for the *keiko gi* that is worn today by exponents of the modern arts of judo, karatedo, and aikido.[4]

Weapons training, as such, receives no emphasis in Tenjin Shinyo-ryu, though several kata involve their use. The weapons used are *bokuto,* or wooden training versions of the *odachi* (long sword) and kodachi (short sword). A few of the techniques that are done with the kodachi are actually meant to be performed with the jutte or iron truncheon. This explains why the torimi will sometimes throw away the short sword after subduing his opponent, and then proceed to choke him or pin him. If the weapon was really meant to be a short sword, this would not be too

---

[4] Exponents of kendo, iaido, naginata, and kyudo continue to wear the older-style training costume of uwagi, obi, and hakama.

sensible, as the tori could more easily, and with less risk to himself, kill his opponent with the blade. If it is supposed to be a method for taking the opponent alive, as a prisoner, though, it becomes more logical from a combative standpoint.

Generally, though, the use of weapons in Tenjin Shinyo-ryu is rudimentary, reflecting an emphasis on unarmed technique presaging the specialization seen in the modern budo, where people train with a single weapon or in unarmed grappling or sparring, to the exclusion of learning the wider variety of weapons skills and combat techniques typical of the classical warrior in preparation for the battlefield. I do not mean to imply that this concentration on unarmed grappling techniques is good or bad. This is merely a recognition of the fact that Tenjin Shinyo-ryu jujutsu, while definitely a classical martial art designed by and for warriors, is an example of how the martial arts have continued to evolve and to adapt to changing conditions. The end of the Tokugawa period was relatively free of organized conflict, and the combative techniques that served on the battlefield were transformed into systems that are more properly seen as methods of self-defense.

Tenjin Shinyo-ryu Jujutsu Today

At the present time, Tenjin Shinyo-ryu has no headmaster. As with several other classical ryuha, a number of shihanke or master teachers, and *ryuha daihyo,* representatives of the tradition, represent the legitimate lines of instruction and authority. In this instance, Iso Mataemon Masayuki, the fifth-generation headmaster, died without leaving any successors, and the Iso family faded out in the Meiji period. Fortunately, however, a number of exponents had received menkyo kaiden licenses from previous headmasters or other teachers, so an unbroken line of qualified teachers, with the authority to issue licenses in their own names, has continued to the present.

Currently, there are several lines of Tenjin Shinyo-ryu. Kubota Toshihiro, a student of Sakamoto Fusataro (of both Tenjin Shinyo-ryu jujutsu and Kodokan judo) received menkyo kaiden in 1973. He established the Tenyokai in June 1978 to continue Sakamoto's teachings, holding a party at the Tojo Kaikan to commemorate the occasion. This event was attended by the headmasters and senior exponents of many different koryu as a signal that they accepted the legitimacy of his position. Kubota has played an active role in teaching both judo and jujutsu over the past twenty-five years and been an active member of the Board of Directors of the Nihon Kobudo Shinkokai (Society for the Promotion of Japanese Classical Martial Arts) and the Nihon Kobudo Kyokai (Japanese Classical Martial Arts Society).

In recent years he has begun to teach some of the resuscitation methods to groups of qualified judo instructors in a series of special seminars in Japan. This was at the urgent request of the Kodokan and the All-Japan Judo Federation, although he was reluctant to do so at first, since the kappo are generally taught only to the most advanced students of Tenjin Shinyo-ryu. Kubota agreed, however, on seeing the need for referees and teachers who are qualified to revive a judoka who has lost consciousness in the course of either training or in a competitive match.

Tobari Kazu headed, until her death some years ago, the lines of Tenjin Shinyo-ryu and Shin no Shinto-ryu that she had learned from her husband, Tobari Takisaburo. Takisaburo studied with Iso Mataichiro, second son of fourth headmaster Iso Mataemon Masanobu, and Inoue Keitaro, a student of Iso Masatomo, the third head of the tradition. His wife, Kazu, ran a small dojo in Osaka and most of her students seemed to be judoka of some ability. They appear, however, to have become rather inactive in recent years and it is unknown if that line of the school's teachings survives.

A third line comes down from Miyamoto Hanzo, who studied with both Inoue Keitaro and Tozawa Tokusaburo, the man who briefly taught jujutsu to Ueshiba Morihei, the founder of aikido. Miyamoto, in addition to being a jujutsu teacher, was also a well-known judoka of the late Meiji, Taisho, and early Showa periods. His top student was Aimiya Kazusaburo, who taught a number of people until he was severely disabled by a stroke about twenty years ago. Of his students, the only one presently teaching is Shibata Koichi, in Saitama Prefecture. Shibata does not appear to be training very actively, and seems to have restricted instruction to people in his immediate family.

CONCLUSION

When the word jujutsu is mentioned, most people probably think of a sort of unarmed grappling that is very similar to the Tenjin Shinyo-ryu. Part of this is due, no doubt, to the influence the school had on Jigoro Kano, the founder of judo, when he created and popularized the art throughout the world from the late Meiji through the early Showa periods. Another reason for this is its very no-nonsense approach. Tenjin Shinyo-ryu may lack the extravagant or flashy techniques of some more recent creations, but it has a very well-founded set of biomechanical and physiological principles that are soundly based on the close observation and extensive empirical knowledge of the realities of close combat. Tenjin Shinyo-ryu can claim to be, without exaggeration, the quintessence of Japanese suhada bujutsu.

References

Fujiwara, R. 1990. *Kakutogi no Rekishi* (History of Combat). Tokyo: Baseball Magazine-sha.

Kawauchi, T. 1954. *Nihon Budo Ryuso-den* (The Lives of the Founders of the Schools of Japanese Martial Arts). Tokyo: Tetsusaburo Kawauchi.

Miyazaki, M., ed. 1994. *Nihon Densho Bugei Ryuha: Dokuhon* (Japanese Traditional Martial Arts Schools: A Handbook). Tokyo: Shin Jimbutsu Oraisha.

Nihon Kobudo Sokan (An Overview of the Japanese Classical Martial Arts). 1988. Tokyo: Shimazu Shobo.

Skoss, M. 1995. Jujutsu and Taijutsu. *Aikido Journal* 22, no. 2:38-39.

Watatani, K. and Yamada, T. 1978. *Bugei Ryuha Daijiten* (Dictionary of Japanese Martial Art Traditions). Tokyo: Tokyo Kopii Shuppanbu.

Liam Keeley was among the first non-Japanese to participate in the Tatsumi-ryu kazunuki, drawing and cutting three thousand times in a single day (see photo on page 149). He has been a member of Tatsumi-ryu since 1984, and has been awarded mokuroku for iaijutsu, kenjutsu, and yawara.

KATO TAKASHI
REFLECTIONS OF THE
TATSUMI-RYU HEADMASTER

Liam Keeley

INTRODUCTION

Kato Takashi, 21st headmaster of the Tatsumi-ryu, was born on July 25, 1913, the second year of the Taisho period; he is now eighty-four years old. He was born in Sakura City, Chiba Prefecture, and went to school there, before going to Kokushikan University. He trained in both kendo and Tatsumi-ryu from a very early age, under the eye of his father, Kato Hisashi, who was a kendo teacher as well as being the 19th headmaster of the Tatsumi-ryu. Apart from this lifelong training in both Tatsumi-ryu and kendo, Kato Sensei also practiced judo and *jukenjutsu* (bayonet fighting) as a young man.

His thorough grounding in martial arts and his strong personal ability led him to be promoted extremely rapidly and within a couple of years he was awarded fourth dan in judo and fifth dan in jukenjutsu.

He was fortunate enough to have had some excellent teachers, including Yamashita Yoshiaki Sensei and Kudo Ichizo Sensei for judo, and Oshima Jikita Sensei for bayonet fighting. When he can be persuaded to reminisce, he is a fount of information of legendary budo figures from the past. He still tells the story about how, after winning a particularly tough judo match, Yamashita Sensei called him over. He ran to his teacher eagerly and made his bow, expecting to be praised, but was cut down by Yamashita Sensei, who said, "Kato, you're strong, but you've got no finesse!"

Kato Sensei and the Tatsumi-ryu are recognized as *mukei bunkazai* (intangible cultural assets) by Chiba Prefecture. He is in great demand as a highly respected and widely experienced teacher of kendo and iai. He is the current president of the Nihon Kobudo Shinkokai (Society

Kato Takashi (right) demonstrating kenjutsu with his son, Hiroshi, at Boso no Mura, Chiba Prefecture, 1991.

for the Promotion of Japanese Classical Martial Arts). He also serves as an adviser to the Board of Physical Education of Sakura City and is a member of the Board of Examiners of the Chiba Prefecture Kendo Federation. For most of his life, Kato Sensei has been a teacher of classical Japanese language. This has been of great value to him in his personal study of the Tatsumi-ryu *makimono,* the scrolls containing information about the *ryu* that are passed down from generation to generation.

TATSUMI-RYU

The Tatsumi-ryu was founded by Tatsumi Sankyo, who is said to have been born in the Eisho period (1504-1520), in what is now Ehime Prefecture, Shikoku. From an early age, Tatsumi Sankyo engaged in strenuous training in the martial arts. As a result, he was never defeated, either on the battlefield or in single combat. He himself, however, was not satisfied with mere technical proficiency, or even victory in combat, and he dedicated himself to the deity Tsumayama Daimyojin in an attempt to go beyond the superficial levels of purely physical achievement.

After arduous training and austere discipline he attained what in Zen terms is known as *satori,* that is, enlightenment arrived at in an intuitive flash of understanding. He then formulated Tatsumi-ryu as a result of his experiences.

KORYU BUJUTSU

The central weapon of the ryu is the sword, and the use of the sword in mortal combat forms the largest part of the curriculum. *Tojutsu*, sword techniques, may be divided into two main divisions, *iaijutsu* (sword-drawing art) and *kenjutsu* (sword art). One of the hallmarks of Tatsumi-ryu is the very high degree of integration between the iai and the kenjutsu techniques, and in fact, at times it is difficult to say which of the two is being performed. There is also a large *yawara* syllabus that covers a wide range of techniques and situations, including the use of a variety of weapons, *katsu* (resuscitation techniques) and *hojojutsu* (art of tying up one's opponent), as well as unarmed combat.

Secondary weapons include the short sword and the spear. The use of a number of other weapons is also taught, not as a specialty, but rather because these weapons were all potential opponents of the sword. Weapons falling into this category are the *bo* (six-foot staff), *naginata* (glaive), and *hanbo* (four-foot staff). In *kata* (prearranged training forms) these weapons "lose" to the sword. Finally, there are a number of weapons for which there are no kata, but which are referred to in the makimono. This category includes the *jutte* (truncheon), *shuriken* (throwing blades), *tessen* (iron fan), and *manrikigusari* (weighted chain). The makimono also include a number of "case studies" of various situations ranging from night fighting and climbing, to esoteric charms and overall strategy.

The connection between the Tatsumi-ryu and Sakura City, in what is present-day Chiba Prefecture, dates back to the 1670s, when the Tatsumi-ryu was recognized as the *otome-ryu* (official style) of the Sakura domain. This 115,000 *koku* (a unit of measurement used to calculate revenues) domain was ruled by the Hotta family from 1745 until the Meiji Restoration of 1868.

At the time of the Restoration a number of famous swordsmen were members of the Tatsumi-ryu. These included Hanzawa Naritsune (18th headmaster of the Tatsumi-ryu), Henmi Sosuke (first head of the kenjutsu training unit of the post-feudal police department), and Kanematsu Naokado. A number of techniques from Tatsumi-ryu were adopted into the police curriculum, including *makiotoshi* from the

omote kenjutsu kata, *shiho* from the *tachiai* iaijutsu, and *tsukagarami* from the yawara syllabus.

An interesting historical sidelight is that Fukuzawa Yukichi (1835-1901), the Meiji period educator and founder of what is today Keio University, whose face also appears on the ¥10,000 note, trained in a branch of the Tatsumi-ryu, known as the Tatsumi

Kato Takashi (right) demonstrating yawara technique in front of a memorial stele dedicated to his father, Hisashi, at Kyozoji Temple, ca. 1975.

Shin-ryu, which was located in the Okudaira domain in Kyushu. Even at the age of sixty, Fukuzawa is said to have practiced iai, performing a thousand draws on such occasions as the New Year. This seems to reflect the Tatsumi-ryu practice of *kazunuki*. On reaching a certain level in the ryu, the trainee may be invited to participate in a special training session in which he will practice the two central techniques of the ryu, *muko* and *marui*, for a total of three thousand draws. Traditionally, this is done at night in the presence of the headmaster, and takes approximately eight hours. It is felt that the essence of the Tatsumi-ryu, as formulated by Tatsumi Sankyo, is contained in these two apparently simple techniques.

INTERVIEW WITH KATO TAKASHI

This interview was conducted in the form of a series of written questions, answered in kind, as Kato Sensei has lost the use of his voice.

Liam Keeley: Kato Sensei, please tell us about your martial arts background.

Kato Sensei: I began my martial arts training with Tatsumi-ryu at the age of six and continued to be taught by my father, Kato Hisashi, until 1948 when he passed away. I continue to pursue my training in Tatsumi-ryu even today.

While the Tatsumi-ryu curriculum focuses primarily on sword techniques (kenjutsu) and sword-drawing (iaijutsu), it is really a comprehensive martial system that also includes grappling (yawara, jujutsu), spear *(sojutsu)*, glaive *(naginatajutsu)*, staff *(bojutsu)*, half-staff *(hanbojutsu)*, throwing spikes and darts *(shurikenjutsu)*, arrest and binding techniques (hojojutsu), group-fighting tactics *(shudan sentoho)*, and scouting techniques *(monomi)*. I have also practiced jukenjutsu (bayonet fighting) and judo.

Where did you do most of your training?

In addition to the dojo at home, which was known as the Yatomi Kendokai, I learned at the Chiba Prefectural Sakura Middle School, at Kokushikan University (where I majored in kendo and Japanese-Chinese Studies), at the Chiba branch of the Dai-Nippon Butokukai, at the Shudogakuin Dojo, and at the Yushinkan Dojo.[1] I received instruc-

---

[1] These dojo were run by two of the most influential swordsmen/kendoka of the prewar era. Shudogakuin was the dojo of Takano Sasaburo (1862-1950), who practiced Ono-ha Itto-ryu, and the Yushinkan was run by Nakayama Hakudo (1873-1958), of the Shindo Munen-ryu.

tion in jukenjutsu at the Toyama Military Academy. In addition to these I have trained in many other places at various times.

What was your motivation for training in martial arts?
I started on the recommendation of my father.

You have trained under many very well-known martial artists. Who among them influenced you most strongly?
My father, Kato Hisashi, 19th headmaster of Tatsumi-ryu, was undoubtedly the strongest influence on me through his guidance in both the spiritual and technical aspects of the Tatsumi-ryu tradition. It was also my good fortune to receive very strict and detailed teaching under several truly great individuals, including Takano Sasaburo, Nakayama Hakudo, Mochida Moriji, Saimura Goro,[2] and Oshima Jikita, all of whom taught me diligently and in their own unique ways. Oshima Jikita was primarily responsible for teaching me jukenjutsu.

CLASSICAL AND MODERN BUDO
Do you think there are any differences between classical and modern budo? Is there any difference, for example, between classical iai and modern iai or kendo or between classical jujutsu and modern judo?
There are both similarities and differences between the two in terms of their content, the kinds of things that are taught in each. In modern budo the emphasis is on physical education and competitive sports, so naturally the dangerous techniques have been removed to prevent injuries. Classical traditions, on the other hand, focus on the undiluted and authentic transmission and teaching of techniques as they were originally designed, to be effective in actual combat situations.

How about the goals and objectives of each?

---

[2] Mochida and Saimura were both 10th dan in kendo.

The goals of classical and modern budo are ultimately the same. However, the process by which those goals are pursued and achieved, in particular the emphasis of the teaching, is usually somewhat different.

Pierre (left) and Claire (center) Simon and Liam Keeley (right) performing kazunuki in Sakura City, January 2, 1992.

How do classical and modern training methods differ?

Here, too, you will find both similarities and differences. In classical budo training we still practice certain techniques designed specifically for their effectiveness in combat, including cuts like *kesagiri* (diagonal cut from shoulder to hip), thrusts to dangerous areas like the *suigetsu* (solar plexus), dislocations of the wrist, knee, and ankle joints, and so on. These have been largely eliminated from modern budo.

Also, in Tatsumi-ryu we have various training methods designed to cultivate, as quickly as possible, freedom of mind and body. For example, practitioners who have attained a certain degree of skill in iai are obliged to perform kazunuki training during which they draw their blade either three thousand times in one day or ten thousand times over a three-day period. We have a similar practice in Tatsumi-ryu kenjutsu called *tachikiri geiko* that involves standing and striking over three thousand times. These represent extremely severe training methods that force practitioners to slip past the boundary of life and death for a time to achieve, in the end, a selfless mental state characterized by great freedom of mind and body. It goes without saying that such extraordinary, strict training methods—which go well beyond anything in ordinary physical education—are not to be found even in the most demanding training sessions of modern budo.

FOREIGN PRACTITIONERS OF CLASSICAL MARTIAL ARTS

What is the most important thing for foreign practitioners in terms of developing a correct understanding of classical Japanese budo?

Foreigners learning such arts are inevitably confronted with a language, culture, and customs different from their own, and to make things easier for them to understand I think the teaching needs to be conducted in a deliberate, conscientious, and unhurried fashion.

What do you find most difficult in teaching your foreign students as opposed to your Japanese students?

One thing I find difficult is to constantly remind myself to use simple words and expressions in order to avoid mistaken interpretations.

Do you make any distinctions between your Japanese and foreign students in terms of your teaching?

No, none at all.

Are there ways in which Japanese and foreign practitioners can help one another in learning classical martial arts?

Yes, there are plenty of ways they can help one another. Such mutual benefit is one of my greatest, most heartfelt desires.

KENJUTSU AND KENDO

You practice both kenjutsu and kendo. How do you keep these two separated in your mind? Do the goals of each differ in any way?

Their goals are ultimately the same.

How about the personalities and attitudes of the practitioners?

I see no differences there, either.

Religion and Spirituality

How are religious traditions such as Zen, esoteric Buddhism, and Shinto related to classical Japanese martial arts?

Zen and Shinto are extremely effective in helping budo practitioners to achieve the mental state that we call *munen muso* (non-ideational thought; literally, no ideas, no desires, no thoughts) that is the fi-

Kato Takashi (right) with one of his kendo instructors, the late Mochida Moriji, ca. 1965.

nal destination of their spiritual training. I view the Shinto and Buddhist deities as symbols of the vast, sublime, omniscient, mysterious Infinite. I would caution, however, that we should be careful to refrain from relying on those deities too much. In the words of Miyamoto Musashi, "Respect the gods, but ask nothing of them." This sums up my perspective on such things quite well. In any case, I confess I know little about religion.

Budo, Life, and the Future

Have you found your experiences learning budo and bujutsu useful in your life in general? How about during the war? In times of peace?

The spiritual state described by the phrase "non-mindedness" (munen muso) and the psychological state of "non-ego" or selflessness (*muga*) that comprise the deepest principles of budo give one a great advantage in making correct decisions and performing correct actions during times of conflict and peace alike. The many years you spend forging yourself spiritually and technically can serve you well in this respect if you find yourself suddenly confronting the unexpected. I believe even now that my training has helped me handle such situations well and in the right way on many occasions.

What role do you think the classical traditions play in Japan today?

Many things forgotten or inadvertently lost over the years from the teachings in modern budo still exist in their original forms within the curriculums of classical traditions. In this sense alone they have great value. In the Confucian *Analects* it says: "By exploring the old, one becomes able to understand the new." I think this sums up the importance of the classical traditions for our modern societies very well.

What do you think of classical martial arts being taught and learned by people abroad?

I think it is a very fine thing, and I hope that the classical martial arts continue to be disseminated abroad on an even wider scale so that people can come to fully appreciate their true richness.

Do you have any worries about the future of modern kendo?

Modern kendo has become an ideal form of physical education and competitive sport, but I think it would be a great loss if it were to become so strongly sport-oriented that interest in its important spiritual and psychological aspects begins to fade.

What are your thoughts, from your vantage point as the current headmaster, on the future of Tatsumi-ryu?

Tatsumi-ryu is a precious cultural asset that has come down to us over a period of nearly five hundred years. I believe strongly that it is my duty to ensure that it continues to exist, and even prosper. Toward that end I hope that Tatsumi-ryu can cultivate many talented practitioners who are capable of carrying on the tradition. My only worry would be if, for some reason, there was no one among those training now, among those who will succeed me, capable of absorbing the whole of what is a very complex and difficult tradition.

Kato Hisashi, 19th Tatsumi-ryu headmaster, performing tameshigiri at the Sakura City Middle School in March, 1937.

Are there any martial artists in history whom you particularly respect and admire?

Tatsumi-ryu founder Tatsumi Sankyo would be one, of course. Also, Niten Ichi-ryu founder Miyamoto Musashi [1584-1645] and Muto-ryu founder Yamaoka Tesshu [1836-1888]. These three in particular I consider to have been great men who, despite the fact that they lived during three entirely different ages, were the highest caliber of human beings. They made some of the greatest strides of any historical figure toward the attainment of true wisdom and enlightenment.

As the president of the Society for the Promotion of Classical Japanese Martial Arts, do you have any message for all the people out there training in budo?

I would again simply quote from the *Analects*, "Harbor not wicked thoughts."

Kato Takashi   153

Ellis Amdur has been teaching Japanese classical martial arts in Seattle since 1989. One of a very few fully authorized instructors outside of Japan, he holds a shihan license, as well the okuden mokuroku, in Toda-ha Buko-ryu, and is licensed as inkajo in Araki-ryu. He is also the author of numerous articles on the classical arts, which have appeared in the Journal of Asian Martial Arts *and* Furyu, *among others.*

KORYU MEETS THE WEST

Ellis Amdur

FOREWORD

The warrior culture of Japan, at its height, was flamboyant (even the humble were flamboyantly so—witness the starving *samurai* picking his teeth when offered food, saying, "No thanks, I just ate,"), grandiose, autocratic, feudal and arrogant. It was predominantly, almost exclusively, male.[1]

I am going to take the tone with which I was taught, the tone with which I teach. My instruction is an amalgam of common knowledge and beliefs, tenets specific to the traditions which I studied, attitudes and opinions inherited from my teacher(s), and things I choose to believe just because I believe them so. All of which I will present as Truth, the Real Deal, the Queen of Our Dreams.

MY BIASED VIEWPOINT TOWARDS KORYU

I will assume that most of my readers have a working knowledge of *ryuha, koryu, bugei*, (martial traditions—all different words for much the same thing). Here's some embellishment. The koryu were organizations that functioned as political entities. Men grouped together to train to acquire power to affect some portion of society. All members wished to be trained fighters, but even more importantly, every member, from highest to lowest, was a servitor. They hired out to serve someone, they inherited a post of service, or if they were *ronin,* ("wave

---

[1] I have written in another place (Amdur 1996) about women in Japanese warrior culture. Therefore, I have no intention of discussing this topic at length here, and in particular, will be bracketing out the rather unusual dynamic of a woman teacher with male students, which I discussed at some length in that article.

men"—meaning someone borne by the currents of life), between jobs, they wandered around looking for someone to serve.

Their focus was on learning how to exert power, including a surgical application of violence, so that their employer and/or their group came out ahead of their enemies. Aside from the fact that they were part of a hereditary military class, something predominant though not exclusive among the koryu in pre-modern times, the best modern equivalents would be such organizations as the Palestine Liberation Front, the Irish Republican Army, the Moro Liberation Front in the Philippines—particularly when such groups go through to a second, even a third generation, passing on methods of violence and group codes of morality and ideology to the younger initiates. We may not like the code of one or another of these groups, and it is equally unlikely that we would have felt comfortable with the moral codes of many of the bugei, particularly in the days when these were not "martial traditions," but were instead, "martial societies."

For example, the lovely phrase, *katsujinken* ("the sword that preserves life") has been used to rationalize all sorts of elegant philosophical treatises bordering on an armed mystical pacifism. The gist of this concept is that you are trained in the use of arms to such an impeccable degree that you can impose your will on others so that they turn from their evil path. It happens sometimes.

The corollary of this expression of will, however, is the implicit sentiment that, "If you don't turn from your evil path, I am prepared to cut you down where you stand." The life that is "preserved" really refers to one's spiritual hands being clean—doing what one has to do for just reasons, for all the lives touched by your actions.

As I am sure the astute reader is well aware, this provides for a lot of leeway. One could be an SS executioner, planting bullets in the backs of Gypsy necks, and feel that, through exterminating vermin to protect the purity of the Aryan nation, one is practicing the sword that preserves life. In other words, it is easy to adopt exotica and assume that not only do you know what they mean, but that the people who created them felt just as you do.

I am not suggesting that samurai were equivalent to Nazis—although some were just as horrible examples of humanity. I am stating that romanticism can be a dangerous thing, and is not sufficient as a means for understanding any sort of aggression, much less organized training for violence.

I believe that we have a difficult, if not impossible task in trying to understand the early practitioners of Japanese martial traditions, be we Japanese or not. Human society has changed to such an incredible degree that much of what we claim to know about our predecessors is mere fantasy. The closest approximation to understanding comes from the inside out, experiences evoked in training, patterned by forcing one's body and mind to the forms of these archaic practices, supplemented by what we can resurrect through the intersection of our imagination with historical writings.

All of this, however, is mediated through the teaching of our instructors, and through theirs, back through time. What we know is that which is seen through the progressive recession of an array of clouded glass, seeing therefore shadows composed as much of our own reflections as a distant sighting of ancient forms.

West Goes to Koryu—and Koryu Goes West

In 1968, I got my jaw dislocated and my nose broken in a fight over honor. My father, a former FBI agent, was too sick with what turned out to be cancer to teach me how to fight himself, so he sent me to a backyard karate school. The style was pretty contrived and silly, a love-child of a few years of Shotokan and gym teacher's fantasy, but somehow, the stories this teacher told and the atmosphere of the training, as pale and white-bread an imitation of a Japanese fighting tradition as it might have been, seized hold of my imagination. Subsequently, after studying several combative arts over the next eight years, I found myself in Japan, intent on staying for two years of solid aikido training. I discontinued aikido after those two years,[2] but I ended up living in Japan for thirteen years, entranced by martial traditions created over four hundred years before aikido and its idealistic principles were ever imagined.

I'd read Donn Draeger's books, and was fascinated by the *idea* of traditional martial arts. Several months into my stay, while living at Kuwamori Dojo, a small family-run aikido school on the outskirts of Tokyo, with only a few words of Japanese under my belt, I happened upon a *dojo* (training hall) practicing Araki-ryu, an extremely rugged method of combat which specialized in close quarters fighting and grappling, with or without weapons.[3] A sinister-looking man in a gray sharkskin suit emerged from the dojo at the startled gasp of the kimono-clad woman student who first met me at the door. The gasp was understandable. What she saw was a shaggy-haired, bearded Caucasian in blue denim jacket and jeans, six feet, six inches tall, trying to look tough while stumbling over a few unintelligible phrases of Japanese. If ever anyone had approached a traditional dojo in an inappropriate fashion, it was I. I bore no gift, I bore no introduction, I wasn't invited, I was dressed like a thug, and I couldn't speak the language.

Many non-Japanese imagine that to enter a traditional martial arts academy, one must approach with impeccable gravity, carrying the perfect gift, speaking elegant formal Japanese, dressed to the nines, bearing introductions from eminent members of society. Even further, some imagine being required to kneel outside the dojo for hours, even days,

---

[2] I returned to practice and teach aikido in 1989. For me, aikido is an aggravating puzzle. I find, however, the struggle provokes me to new perspectives in ways that I would never have come to had I stayed *exclusively* with the martial traditions I found and still find more congenial. See my articles in *Aiki News/Aikido Journal*, starting with issue #96, 1993, for a variety of perspectives on both aikido and other combative arts.

[3] Actually, my fellow contributor Meik Skoss first noticed the school practicing at a gymnasium on his way to the barbershop, and later told me about it. Given that he maintained a brush cut barely half an inch in length, I never figured out why he had to go several train stops to get his hair cut, but I'm eternally grateful that he did.

before receiving permission to enter. Of course, knowing polite behavior is to be preferred, and fluent Japanese, good clothing, and introductions from reputable members of society are really the best way to go (please don't imitate me, in other words), but in the final analysis, it comes down to one human being meeting another and finding, face-to-face, mutual respect and interest beyond the confinement of culture. (The closest I ever came to the "sitting outside the temple in the rain for days" fantasy was being required to maintain a low horse stance for forty-five minutes before being admitted to the Nation of Islam kung fu school run by George HX in New Haven, Connecticut.)

The man in the suit, lean and rather tall for a Japanese, calmly looked up at me and asked why I was there. I eventually was able to explain that I wanted to watch practice. He replied that they let no one watch practice. Struggling to put me in context, he did the Japanese thing—he tried to find an affiliation, a group or individual with whom I was associated. He asked if I knew Donn Draeger, a man he respected. I knew who he was, and I tried to convey my knowledge by saying, "Yes, Mr. Draeger is the mentor of foreign practitioners of martial arts." What I said, however, was, "*Hai, Draeger-san wa watakushi no obasan*" ("Yes, Mr. Draeger is my aunt"). With remarkable aplomb, my interlocutor blinked once and resumed his calm gaze up at me.

He said, "Do you want to do koryu?" What he meant was, "Do you want to do Araki-ryu?"

I, not understanding, said, "Yes." What I meant was, "Yes, I want to do koryu, specifically Yagyu Shinkage-ryu which I intend to visit tomorrow. That's really an elegant sword art, with a remarkable, romantic history! I think Araki-ryu is too rough and crude, what with photos of old men wrapping chains around each other's necks and flinging each other through the air by those chains. But I do want to watch *you* do it."

He invited me in. I did something right. I went to a corner, and sat quietly on my knees for three hours, legs simultaneously asleep and screaming. I asked no questions, gaped no yawns, and I watched—very intently. After the class, the instructor came up to me and said, "You can start next week." I had not realized that I had also made a decision when I replied, "Thank you, I will."

One can be forgiven not knowing the nuances of the etiquette of a foreign culture, but of universal value to those in martial societies are a willingness to maintain one's dignity in the face of pain and fatigue, and the ability to wait—to refrain from intrusive questions that are really for the purpose of calling attention to oneself.

Years later, he told me, "You walked up, and I couldn't understand a word you said, so I looked in your eyes. I've met more than a few Americans, and I could tell you were a very weird American. I figured, 'I'm a really weird Japanese, so it might be interesting to have you around.'"

In 1978, I also entered the Toda-ha Buko-ryu, a school which specializes in the use of the *naginata* (a glaive—a sword-like blade mounted on a long shaft; see my articles in the *Journal of Asian Martial Arts*). Although it is quite common for non-Japanese living in Japan to enter more than one ryuha, this is a very complex enterprise, and it is often a mistake. With enough practice, one can master the movements of more than one system, but often, at heart, one is merely doing "generic koryu," becoming a master of movement without appreciating, much less comprehending, the heart of each system.

Thinking back to my own studies, I found it an exceedingly arduous task to maintain my studies in two martial traditions.[4] Because of my primary commitment, at that time, to the Araki-ryu, my study of Toda-ha Buko-ryu suffered. I grew quite good at going through the movements of the latter, but it was only in my twelfth year of training that I could honestly say that I was *doing* Toda-ha Buko-ryu, that it had finally sunk into my bones.

---

[4] I also did quite a bit of cross-training in those years, studying judo, *hsing-i ch'uan* (a powerful form of Chinese boxing), Thai kickboxing, and *t'ai chi ch'uan*, but these were really for the purpose of supplementing my core study of Araki-ryu. I was quite honest with myself in my lack of full commitment to each of these supplementary disciplines. I trained in these more modern forms to pick up skills—I never could refer to myself, for example, as a *judoka* (practitioner of judo) or a kickboxer.

I think of it as similar to committing fully to two families, two wives. Koryu do not only differ in the nature of their movements. The organizing principles, the methods of psychological training, the character of the system and the quality of personality that each creates within an individual are radically different (or should be, unless the ryu has degenerated into a mere collection of physical training exercises). Without an almost insane level of commitment to two or more masters, it is a mistake, wasting both one's own time and disrespectful to both the traditions and their teachers.

When I returned to America, one of the first errors I made was to allow several people to simultaneously enter both ryuha. This was a good choice for one man, although he will surely take far longer to master each school than if he were to study just one. However, with a solid base of nearly thirty years in a variety of combative arts, he seems to have the capacity to maintain his focus and attention in these two very different traditions. The other people who attempted dual study no longer practice either school—I eventually told each of them that they would have to choose, as I was spending each practice correcting their mistakes, which were really "contamination" of the technical and attitudinal criteria of the other ryu. Truly bound to neither, they chose to leave. I will never allow this dual training again.

Flowing from the Past

My Araki-ryu instructor considered the word *kobudo* (old martial way, the most common word used to refer to classical martial traditions) to be anathema. Many koryu have been awarded the appellation of "intangible cultural treasure" *(mukei bunkazai)*, on a local or even prefectural level. Curling his lip with scorn, my teacher would say, "'Kobudo.' In other words, something fixed and dead, like an antique. Add to that 'intangible cultural treasure,' and you have the equivalent of moldy museum pieces. Look at the museum! They have those pathetic stuffed tigers. If posed well, you get a sense of what their power might have been, but how does that compare to the living beast in his jungle? We don't do kobudo. We practice *koryu budo*."

This phrase means a martial practice that flows from the past into the present. In other words, it still develops, it still lives, *it still exerts influence on the world.*

Parenthetically, I might mention that Donn Draeger's formulation of *bujutsu* (martial arts/techniques) and *budo* (martial ways) was regarded by my instructor, and in fact, by most Japanese, with bemusement when it was presented and amusement when it was explained. Araki-ryu, for example, which is surely one of the crudest and roughest of koryu, with a savage attitude towards combat, always referred to itself as a budo. For most Japanese involved in such practices, there was not a clear distinction between self-perfection and self-protection. One could become "enlightened" with blood on one's hands. Draeger made much of the selfless nature of the oldest martial traditions, in which one trained and fought for a social nexus rather than for oneself, opposing it to the more individualistic pursuit of self-perfection in his definition of budo. However, the very concept of "oneself" is uniquely Western. The ideas of non-attachment, of the "emptiness of the self" (i.e., transitory nature of personal identity) are much more readily understood in societies like Japan, which never attempted to develop the individual self to the extent that we in the West have done. Many of the arts that are called budo in Draeger's work are simply martial traditions that either became enervated and unrealistic during the hundreds of years of totalitarian peace in the Edo period (1602-1867), or were founded in this period by individuals who had never seen combat of any kind, much less a field of battle, and thus their combative arts became an amalgam of solid knowledge, philosophy, and fantasy.

Japanese certainly understand the nuances of the words bujutsu and budo, when the two are used in conversation. Yet I have heard pugnacious individuals dismiss martial systems like aikido with the phrase, "That's not budo." Only in America have I ever heard the phrase, "That's not bujutsu."

For the Japanese, anything can be a "way" of being, even that of the bloodiest warrior, particularly if he devotes his life to something greater than himself. *Bushido*, the way of the warrior, is, by definition, a way of living selflessly, in service to another, be it person or cause.

The line of Araki-ryu that I practiced was true to its own definition of koryu. Even the oldest *kata* (forms) were ruthlessly examined with an attempt to make them more effective while still retaining the essential character of the school. In addition, new forms and freestyle practice were developed for modern day self-defense, street fighting or combat with improvised weapons. This included practice in methods of unarmed *kakuriki* (grappling) and *kempo* (striking with hands and feet). Such innovation was not something particular to this generation. Araki-ryu has always adjusted and adapted to local conditions in each generation and location that it alighted, in keeping with its defining phrase, *"Ichi koku, ichi den:* In each country/location, one tradition." My instructor used to say, "If you return to America and simply teach what I taught you, I will consider you a failure. America is different—you will have to teach Amdur-ryu. Call it Araki-ryu if you like, but it will have to be developed so it suits you, and suits your country." This statement might be at variance with the rigidly conservative attitudes of many of the koryu, but in fact, he, and subsequently I, regarded them as of a different breed, preservation societies rather than living martial systems. However, unlike purely utilitarian fighting styles such as the so-called Brazilian jiu-jitsu of the Gracie family, Araki-ryu has never merely pruned what is not immediately relevant to local conditions. Instead, it has tried to maintain a delicate balance between the practice of old weaponry, appropriate to the needs of the ancient time of its origin, and the study of methods of combat appropriate to modern times—all, however, imbued with the same essential spirit. For me, any Araki-ryu movement is instantly recognizable, like the silhouette of a family member caught for a second passing through the shadows. Thus, koryu—flowing from the past.

At approximately year eleven of my stay, my Araki-ryu instructor told me to write out the *kishomon* (vow on entering the ryu). Some traditions have the person do this on the date of entry. Araki-ryu does this on the day one is given *inkajo* (literally "rank of the seal," meaning one has authority to pass on the tradition). One writes out a series of vows, including such things as under what conditions one will duel, vows of secrecy, promises of respect to one's instructor, then signs and "seals" it with one's blood *(keppan),* promising that if any of these vows are broken, you will accept the horrible punishment of, in Araki-ryu's case, an array of Buddhist deities.

I had never studied calligraphy—and my knowledge of written Japanese was poor; however, I began, nightly, with brush and ink, to write the characters of the vows. After six months, I had a copy that had no blots. I proudly brought it to my instructor; he perused it, and said, "You know, if my first-grader came home with this, I'd be so proud! Good block letters, Amdur-san!" A small silence. "But calligraphy should express the personality of the writer. This has none... unless this reflects who you are?"

Years passed. I continued to write nightly, with emotions antithetical to those necessary to practice either martial arts or calligraphy. I was irritated, under pressure, tense, frustrated. Every six months or so, I would bring another copy. One day, I achieved the dubious praise, "If my kid in junior high came home with this..." and then my teacher finally looked at me and said, "Picasso, that's what I'm looking for! Picasso."

I thought, "What the hell is that supposed to mean?" and more or less abandoned writing altogether. I thought about it at times, kicking myself for not taking calligraphy lessons or studying more Japanese, yet at the same time grumbling that I hadn't come to Japan to study penmanship!

I finally decided that it was time to return to America. I had no career in Japan—the best I could claim for myself was that I was a minor curiosity to a small circle of people—a foreigner with some skill in antiquated martial traditions. Aside from my family, I could take pride in no accomplishment but my skill at a hobby, because, having no utility in my life, that is all I could really call my martial training. According to my Araki-ryu instructor, one trained to create within oneself the skills and power to move a portion of the world in some fashion that both challenged one's moral courage and put oneself at risk—out on the edge. If one did not, one was a "salaryman budoka." As a junior high English teacher, I felt the latter described me perfectly. I was ashamed of my own life.

I decided to return home to America, to get an education and specialize in crisis intervention—to use my skills in a unique way so that I might better meet my teacher's eyes someday; not as an "equal" (for he would always be a generation "ahead" of me), but as one who was true to what he had been taught, and to the example of the man who taught me, as different as his expression of that power was.[5]

My ties were quite deep with my teachers, and it was very difficult for me to reject the further instruction that they offered. I was saying, in effect, that I believed that I could best perfect my art elsewhere than in their presence. I think of *musha shugyo,* the period when a young warrior left his teacher and toured around, engaging in training and challenge matches, as similar to my situation. There is a time that continued presence with one's teacher serves no more than to make one a better student. One has to leave. There is, however, often disagreement as to when is the right time to leave, but this act of minor rebellion is also in keeping with a step away from the circle of the "family."

Loyalty is one of the cardinal characteristics of studying koryu. This loyalty is fostered in part by the method of training—in practicing the "losing" side in kata practice, one's teacher actually puts himself at risk on your behalf. Any increase in skill and insight is, therefore, due to his sacrifice. A peculiar intimacy builds up over the years, peculiar because it is a product of the sense of indebtedness, trust, and admiration that builds after many years of dancing with fear, anger, and the potential of both dying and dealing death, as well as the irritation and friction that

---

[5] My koryu training is thus legitimized for me in my current work as owner of a company called Edgework. Most of my work deals with the de-escalation of the violent or suicidal, in calming agitated mentally ill individuals, and in training others how to do the same. The continued practice of koryu budo is validated for me in my use of its principles (and more esoteric techniques) in daily life, sometimes in a situation of some risk. Without such work, I would feel absurd in ongoing practice as I would find myself going through the motions of something totally alien to my own life. I wish to make it quite clear that I have no interest in why others might practice koryu; simply that such an attitude was bequeathed to me in my own lineage, and that is how I judge myself.

increasingly generates heat as one is brought face-to-face with the inevitable flaws that are revealed in this person whom you admire so much. There is a secondary tension, between one's loyalty to the tradition and teacher opposed by the surging energy, the blood bubbling within you, urging you out to make your own mark on the world. For many, this tension is resolved by either a bitter or stupid resignation to being a good follower, a man who does what he is told. In times of peace, this creates stagnation and backbiting among the ryu's members, something quite common among many koryu in Japan today; in times of war, such men do what they are told, having never measured their moral sensibilities against the strictures of their leader/teacher. For others, the tension becomes intolerable—leading to rebellion or simply quitting. My two closest friends in the Araki-ryu, the last two other than myself of my generation, both left after almost a decade each, suddenly—the psychological demands had become intolerable.

Other people, more fortunate, in more benign schools, form a small community, a momentary "village," in which one is part of a group happy to simply practice together, with no larger goal in mind.

What is most difficult is to maintain the tension, walking the tightrope, loyal in the largest sense to both the teacher and the ryuha, without compromise of one's morals or one's destiny. Paradoxically, the only way I could do this was to leave.

This loyalty is neither a Japanese nor an American trait. The sincere devotion of one person to another, an implicit confidence, were it to come to such extremity, that each would "cover the other's back," coupled with a clear-eyed view of one's teacher's virtues and flaws is not culturally bound. I tried to embody this to the best of my ability, and I have been lucky enough to have found such men among my own students. Their devotion is not blind—not only are they aware of my flaws, but they let me know of them too—yet their respect is real, and all the more treasured because of its realism.

A week before I left for America, my Araki-ryu teacher and I went to a mountain lodge and for three days trained ten hours a day, drank beer half the night, and trained again. The night before I left for this trip, I remembered Picasso. I grabbed a brush and ink and paper and thought,

"Picasso he wants; Picasso he gets." I literally scribbled the kishomon in a welter of swirls, a few with their own accidental symmetry, others a jagged blur of black on white. Perhaps more Jackson Pollack than Picasso, but it was the best I could do.

After the first day of training, we were sitting in our room, in lightweight summer kimono, drinking bottle after bottle of Kirin beer, and judging the time right, I slipped the rolled paper out of my backpack, and in smooth and subtle Japanese (no "Donn Draeger's my aunt" for this boy now!) said, "I prepared this uninteresting bit of stuff. Perhaps you might want to have a glance at it…" He unrolled it, and looked it over very carefully. He drained his beer glass, which I immediately filled, and he took another sip, slow and contemplative. "You know, if you ever had understood that this was not necessary, you'd really deserve inkajo," and he carefully rolled it up and handed it back to me.

I burst out roaring with laughter, saying, "I know, that's what I've been thinking for two years, but I did it anyway! I've felt like such an idiot, cursing myself out, cursing you out." He laughed with me as I cavalierly stuffed it back in my pack. We went on drinking half the night, talking of other things.

After two more days of practice, we were again drinking, and the subject returned to the kishomon. I laughed again, for I felt both ridiculous, and an enormous relief. I told how I had tried to commandeer my then-wife's drawing table—but she, an artist, kicked me off, saying she didn't lend the table to anyone and that my anxiety about this budo stuff was pretty pathetic, and so I ended up at the dining room table, which still bore blotches of ink. He laughed with me, and then said, "Let me have another look at it." I rooted around in my backpack, and found it in the bottom, crumpled into a ball. He smoothed it out, read it again, and folding it carefully, put it in the sleeve of his kimono, saying, "I'll keep this as a souvenir."

Teaching Koryu in the West

So I returned to the United States with license to teach. In the Toda-ha Buko-ryu, this was very traditional—I was appointed *shihan* (full instructor) in the presence of instructors of other ryu as witnesses in a formal ceremony; in the Araki-ryu, it was, as I have described—unique.

Now I was stuck. I never really desired to teach—I merely wished to continue to train, and to make it a training that contributed to the real business of living. But you make a contract with your teachers when you enter a koryu, particularly when a school bears the weight of generations. You must not let the tradition die, thereby betraying all of your teachers, who struggled to pass the school down to you. You are personally responsible for its survival and its future. You alone.

It took me about a year to get my rhythm straight, to stop thinking in Japanese when caught off guard. My second day in America, I went to buy a car. I went to a used-car lot, and a skinny guy in polyester with a pencil mustache and slicked back hair asked me my name.

"Amdur," I said.

"What's your first name?" he asked.

Thinking he must need it for some potential paperwork, I replied, "Ellis."

"Well Ellis, my man, have I got a deal for you."

I almost jumped down his throat. The only conceivable reason I could imagine for a lowly car salesman to use my first name was to purposely degrade me. I stopped myself in mid-turn, remembering I was no longer in Japan, and people in this strange country did things differently.

I started teaching Araki-ryu in 1989. Having no idea if I would be successful or not, I decided to build a "firewall" between my new students and the tradition I valued so much. Therefore, I created five new sword-drawing forms. My goals were to create forms fully congruent with the technical criteria of the school, which could function as exercises to create the musculature and reflexes needed to accommodate its techniques. The students would be building skills that would be necessary to learning the traditional forms of Araki-ryu. On the other hand, if my students drifted away after a year or so, they would do so without having any of the "family heirlooms," but only what I had added myself. Over time, I gradually introduced the more modern components of the ryu, the grappling and kempo, and only after yet another year, the first of the traditional forms.

Perhaps ten or fifteen men gave the school a try. A little while after I started teaching Araki-ryu, I also began teaching the Toda-ha Buko-ryu. At the time of this writing, I have three students in Araki-ryu and four in Toda-ha Buko-ryu.

One difficulty I have found in teaching in the States is my students' level of commitment. I gauge others based upon my perception and memory of my own training. I literally put my life on hold, in some respects, to study koryu. In thirteen years in Japan, I took almost no vacations, I did not build a career there, and my life centered around my practice. I not only trained on the days of practice (no more than once or twice a week per ryu), but almost every day on my own. Injured, I would sit quietly month after month, observing class. I paid dues to the dojo even when I was out of the country for months at a time. I would get up at midnight and practice sword drawing on the grounds of a Shinto shrine. I went over kata in my mind repetitively as I drove to work or rode the train, and when afflicted by insomnia, rather than count numbers or sheep, would again rehearse forms in tiny detail on the screen of my closed eyelids. I would consciously experiment with the methods of exerting one's will on others (called *kiaijutsu*), in the course of my daily activities. I would orient my mind and my practice around one or another of the *okuden* (deep transmissions)—esoteric, cryptic phrases that illustrated essential principles of each school. For example, I would take the phrase, "Old snow laden pine tree on a cliff face, immovable for one thousand years," and try to embody the tenacity, the twisted, sinewy "bedamn'd to the ice, the wind, and the pain" grit of that phrase, and imbue every movement with its character, making it a part of me.

I miss that obsessional, perhaps slightly insane level of commitment in my students. As I explained to one man, "For you, this tradition is like pepper, to make the meal more interesting; for me, it was always the food by which I survived." I don't fault any of my students for choosing how much they want to learn, but there is a sadness, too, because I could give them much more.

Another difference between the style of American and Japanese practitioners of martial arts is occasional "arguments about rectitude." People imagine koryu dojo as immensely formal places where one walks on pins-and-needles. One of the silliest scenes I have ever seen has been the made-in-America-dubious-lineage "koryu," with obsequious students sweatily tiptoeing among arrogant, pompous seniors and instructors, speaking pseudo-Japanese-accented English in ridiculous imitations of fantasy samurai. Every true koryu dojo I have ever been in has had the laughter of men-at-arms, rude jokes and informal etiquette, with instantaneous shifts to formality or to fighting mode when it is called for. The nervous tension of the former kind of school is absolutely antithetical to any genuine training of a fighting warrior in which the conservation of energy is as important as its expenditure.

Nonetheless, it surprises me again and again when I correct an individual and he replies, "But you said last week..." or "Why," or "I don't think so, how about if I..."[6] One example that really torques my jaws occurs while I am functioning as *uke* (literally "receiver," the person in a two person form in the teaching/senior position). In the middle of the form, I realize that I am about to strike/cut/injure my partner, and I abbreviate the attack. At the conclusion of the form, I point out the error. On a few occasions, a student has said, "I don't think so. I could have blocked/avoided/gotten you first." There is, I confess, a temptation to show the individual where they are mistaken—graphically, forcefully. My predecessors of previous eras would have done so without guilt or hesitation. Instead, I point out that there would be only one way to prove me right or wrong. "I would strongly advise that you take my word for it—next time I am not going to pull the blow, and if you do not do it in this manner (demonstrating the correct way), you will get hurt, and I honestly don't want to hurt you." Then I do attack

---

[6] A running joke in the dojo has been what I would title this essay. Some are unprintable, but one which made it to the "final drawing" was "But, but, but, you never told us that before."

Koryu Bujutsu

full force. Thankfully, my students have chosen to trust me and move correctly. Even more thankfully, it has been many years since I have had to engage in this particular discussion.

I distinguish this rectitude argument from open questions like, "How would this work against someone who used short punches, an in-fighter, as opposed to a long-range boxer?" The questions I find objectionable are faintly argumentative, or serve the purpose of proving the questioner right or knowledgeable. They are not an honest search for information.

When I began teaching, I was more tolerant of this, thinking that I needed to fit in with American culture, but I later found this to be a mistake. I was doing my students a disservice, robbing them of the chance to learn by doing rather than saying. So now I reply, "Yeah, I lied last week," or "I'll change my mind again next week," or "You need to stop trying to show me what you know and come here to learn," or "I really don't care what you think, you don't know enough about this movement to make a comparison. Learn it first, then we'll talk." And increasingly, silent body language, anything from a raised eyebrow to simply walking away.

What the student must remember is that even if they are "right," they cut off further discourse by insisting on proving that they are. If a student claims "I did that," when being corrected, I have no interest in interacting further with them. If they merely *think* it, while thanking me for my suggestion, they can use my perhaps slightly inaccurate observation (maybe my angle of vision was wrong) as a confirmation of their attainment.

I judge my students on what they can do, and on how many times I must correct them for the same thing. Re-educating oneself away from an incorrect movement and coordinating an effective reflexive action can take hundreds, even thousands of repetitions—if my student returns the next week with the same mistake intact, I know how much he has practiced.

A corollary to this sort of exchange is hurt feelings. I believed that when my instructors in Japan no longer criticized me, they had lost interest in me. I hated correction as I, shamed, found another of my flaws revealed to the light—flaws that I either did not want revealed or didn't even know that I had. However, I knew that I was not training to gain approval or praise—I deliberately entered my study to be torn apart, not shored up. I had enough confidence in my own core that I regarded criticism as a gift, a harsh, sometimes deeply painful gift when another chunk of ego got ripped lose. This has been a hard thing to convey to a few of my students. I believe that since Japanese students expect to learn in this manner, such criticism is experienced as far less damaging, and thus, taken far less personally than by some Americans.

Nishioka Tsuneo, master instructor of Shinto Muso-ryu jojutsu said to me in a conversation that for him, the modern-day equivalent of *hamon* (expulsion from a ryu) is to ignore a student who offends him. They are welcome to practice in his dojo, but he will either completely neglect them, or with utter dispassionate indifference "praise" them, saying, "Fine, that's very good. Carry on."

A few years ago, two eminent instructors of another ryu visited my dojo. Several of my students were quite inept that night, stage-frightened because of the guests, and also evidencing that they had not trained regularly in quite some time. Finally, I told them that I was quite bored teaching the same thing over and over again, and sent them off to the side, telling them to practice the initial basic movements of the tradition which they still hadn't acquired after three years. I spent the rest of the practice working with my senior student.

I discussed this at length after class, going so far as to say that perhaps I was mistaken in my intention to teach the complete curricula of the tradition, with its many weapons and techniques. "Given your slow progress, and incredible attachment to the same damn mistakes, maybe it would be best for each of you to select your favorite weapon, and I'll only teach you those forms. At your current rate of training, in particular, one weapon alone would be a lifelong training."

One of the students, deeply offended, gradually stopped coming to class. Another confronted me. He is an excellent teacher of a modern martial art, and he felt that my harshness served to tear him and his fellows down. He pointed out that I had few students, and with my callous and insulting attitude, would possibly lose the few I had, that he had made considerable efforts to find the best way to teach each of his own students, finding out their strong and weak spots, building them up rather than tearing them down, and that finally, it was a terrible shame that something as valuable as what I had to offer was held so narrowly, taught in an elitist manner to so few.

I replied that I think the way he teaches his students is admirable, and that, in fact, when I teach aikido, I try to do so in the same way, but that koryu is different. I continued to explain that although I liked him very much, it was a matter of complete indifference to me were he to walk out the door that day never to return. "You see, I *am* Araki-ryu. I'm all you get, the only way there is to do it. There are no other teachers from whom you can get another viewpoint. In that sense, what I have to offer is 'perfect.' There can be no question, at your level, of another way to do things, because you can't do with your body or mind what I do, which is what you came to me requesting to learn. When you can do it, you'll be your own instructor and you can change the thing any way you damn well please. You would have a right to combine it with tango lessons or hip-hop or some silly American kung fu system. I might not like it, but if you receive a teaching license, you will be expected to imbue the system with yourself. However, not before that time; not now. I respect you, I like you, and as a human being, we are equal. In many areas of life, I'm sure that you are far ahead of me. But here, we are not equal, I'm steps above you, and I cannot teach you, one friend to another. I'm not here for an exchange. You are here to learn something that can only be learned vertically, top to bottom, because you have to be willing to open yourself to being wrong, time and time again. Now if I am ever abusive, then to hell with me, throw me by the side of the road, and go on your way, but harsh teaching is not abusive in itself." He is still with me, still struggling at times, but still there.

However, despite my authoritarian attitudes, I do not accept my students calling me "*sensei*" inside or outside of the dojo. We live in America, and my name is Ellis, at least for people with whom I am closely acquainted. We laugh and joke in the dojo, and in freestyle grappling or kempo, my students, all seasoned martial artists in their own right, sometimes beat me. If I needed a title to earn authority, obsequious students uttering honorifics as they rush to fold my clothes or pour me beer, if I needed to set up practice so that I never lose, then I would be a coward and would have no right to teach. There is a hierarchy, based on the fact that I am standing on the shoulders of eighteen generations of predecessors, and I have earned my place there, at the cost of a few broken bones, bruises, and painful struggle with both my teachers and my own self. It is no more necessary that my students bow and scrape or that I am falsely believed to be "invincible," than it was that Angelo Dundee be able to beat Muhammed Ali to coach him in boxing.

I have noticed other differences between students East and West. Japanese students tend to observe in a quieter, perhaps more intuitive way. If they notice people, particularly seniors, cleaning up, they begin to clean too. If everyone is practicing one type of form and they are late, they will simply begin to practice the form themselves. Time and time again, I find myself, in America, realizing that I have to make an explicit request or order for others to pick up on what I am doing.

American students tend to try to depend more on a verbal *and* a visual understanding. It is quite common for them to practice in front of a mirror, to ask lots of questions, and to finally "get it." I find that more than very occasional use of mirrors extinguishes one's ability for "insight."

Until modern times, no one practiced with mirrors. You learned through a physical awareness of your orientation in space, in concrete success and failure in kata training, in various forms of sparring and in combat, and finally, through the instruction and example of your teacher. Your mirror was not silvered glass—your looking glass was the man with whom you studied. His actions, words and example became a reflection of what you were trying to become. At once mirror and lens, he illuminated your flaws in both technique and character simply by highlighting the difference between who you were, who you wished to believe yourself to be, and who you could become, were you to practice with enough heart to become a "reflection" of him. Not a copy, however. One reflected the essence of the ryu as embodied in the teacher and then in yourself, still remaining yourself, and yet utterly changed in the process. In this endeavor, looking at oneself in a mirror on the wall plays a very trivial part.

Despite their greater ease of understanding the essentials of training in koryu, however, the vast majority of Japanese koryu students, in my experience, are rather casual hobbyists. Very few of them are individuals whom I would want to guard my back on the field of battle, in an alleyway, or even during a verbal confrontation at my job. The koryu, in Japan, are, for the most part, as my teacher criticized earlier—kobudo: antiques, old curiosities.

There are many nuances to Japanese culture that even the most casual Japanese student will know "without knowing"—it is just the way people act, as far as they are concerned. Japanese culture permeates koryu, and they were created to be learned in a Japanese fashion. That non-Japanese are unaware of many of these nuances is natural and of no great concern. Such nuances can be taught. Thus, all of the above criticisms of non-Japanese practitioners are simply a matter of education, just as the techniques of sword and stave. It is only when someone refuses to accept this that they are unsuited to enter a koryu.

The people who stay in this utterly alien activity, an anachronism in Japan, an anomaly in America, are rather remarkable individuals. I have found that among my students are people with the capacity to enter into another world view, with the courage to allow it to enter them. They are, frankly, hungrier and more sincere that the average Japanese student, even if they have to be taught things that Japanese drink in with their mothers' milk. Finally, these men truly do approach these koryu as combative arts—by learning "as if" they are preparing for war, they challenge themselves spiritually much as they would were they actually training for the battlefield. We put our lives on the line, not in duels and fights, but in what we risk in the process of learning where we truly stand in this odd arena of violence bound in archaic tradition. In the process, we become family to each other, and thus, truly members of the ryu.

References

Amdur, E. 1995. The Development and History of the Naginata. *Journal of Asian Martial Arts* 4, no. 1.

———. 1996. The Role of Arms-Bearing Women in Japanese History. *Journal of Asian Martial Arts* 5, no. 2:10-35.

Draeger, D.F. 1973b. *Classical Budo.* The Martial Arts and Ways of Japan, 2. New York & Tokyo: Weatherhill.

———. 1973a. *Classical Bujutsu.* The Martial Arts and Ways of Japan, 1. New York & Tokyo: Weatherhill.

———. 1974. *Modern Bujutsu & Budo.* The Martial Arts and Ways of Japan, 3. New York & Tokyo: Weatherhill.

Pranin, S., and D. Skoss, eds. 1994-. *Aikido Journal.* Vol. 21-. Tokyo: Aiki News.

GLOSSARY

A

aiki 合気 unified energy

aikido 合気道 way of aiki; a modern martial art derived from jujutsu

aikijutsu 合気術 techniques of aiki

aite 相手 opponent

Asayama Ichiden-ryu 浅山一伝流 classical comprehensive martial of the goshi

ashigaru 足軽 foot soldiers; the lowest level of bushi

atarashii naginata 新なぎなた lit., new naginata; modern martial art of naginata

atemi 当身 strike

atemiwaza 当身技 techniques of striking

B

bakufu 幕府 military government of Japan

battojutsu 抜刀術 techniques of sword-drawing; sword-drawing art

bo 棒 staff

bojutsu 棒術 techniques of the staff; staff art

bokuto 木刀 wooden sword

budo 武道 martial ways

bugei 武芸 martial arts

bujutsu 武術 martial arts, martial techniques

bushi 武士 Japanese warrior

bushido 武士道 way of the bushi, or Japanese warrior

C

Chokugen-ryu onaginatajutsu 直元流大長刀術 classical tradition that specializes in the use of a very large naginata

D

Dai Nippon Butokukai 大日本武徳会 Greater Japan Martial Virtues Society

dan 段 lit. step; indicates a degree of black belt

densho 伝書 transmission documents of a classical ryu

deshi 弟子 disciple, student

dojo 道場 lit. way place; a place where martial arts are practiced

doshin 同心 Tokugawa period law enforcement official

F

fudoshin 不動心 imperturbable or immovable spirit

fukuro shinai 袋撓 training sword made of bamboo encased in leather

furibo 振棒 heavy training club used in Jikishinkage-ryu to develop proper technique and stamina

furisode 振袖 long-sleeved kimono worn by young unmarried women

furui 古い old

G

gokui 極意 hidden or secret; in Yagyu Shinkage-ryu, one of the okugi techniques

go no sen 後の先 responsive initiative; also machi no sen

goshi 郷士 farmer warriors; bushi who held and worked land

gunbaisha 軍配者 practitioner of battlefield divination

H

habiki 刃引 metal-bladed sword; can be sharp or rebated

hachidan 八段 8th degree black belt

hachimaki 鉢巻 headband

hachiwari 鉢割 helmet-splitter

hakama 袴 pleated divided skirt or culottes

hakuda 白打 unarmed close-combat techniques

hamon 破門 formal expulsion from a ryu

hanbo 半棒 short staff

hanbojutsu 半棒術 techniques of the short staff

hanshi 範士 master-level instructor

heiho 兵法 martial principles or military strategy

hikitate geiko 引立稽古 training to improve someone's technical skill or level

hinawaju 火縄銃 matchlock musket

hojo 捕縄 binding and securing

hojojutsu 捕縄術 binding techniques, using a tying cord to restrain prisoners

Hokushin Itto-ryu kenjutsu 北振一刀流剣術 classical sword tradition

hyoho 兵法 see heiho

I

iaido 居合道 way of sword-drawing; a modern martial art

iaijutsu 居合術 techniques of sword-drawing; sword-drawing art

inkajo 印可状 lit. rank of the seal; authority to pass on the tradition

Itto Shoden Muto-ryu kenjutsu 一刀正伝無な流剣術 classical sword tradition

J

jigeiko 地稽古 free practice or sparring in kendo, atarashii naginata, jukendo

jita kyoei 自他共栄 mutual benefit and welfare

jo 杖 stick, usually about four feet in length

jojutsu 杖術 techniques of the stick; stick art

judo 柔道 way of flexibility; modern martial art

judogi 柔道着 jacket and trousers worn while doing judo

jujutsu 柔術 techniques of flexibility; grappling art

jukendo 銃剣道 way of the bayonet; modern martial art

jukenjutsu 銃剣術 techniques of the bayonet; bayonet art

jutte 十手 single-tined truncheon

K

kabutowari 兜割 helmet-splitter

kaeshiwaza 返技 techniques to reverse or escape techniques being applied to oneself

kamae 構 engagement posture

kami 神 Shinto diety or dieties

kappo 活法 resuscitation methods or techniques

karatedo 空手道 way of the empty hand; modern martial art

Kashima Shinden Jikishinkage-ryu 鹿島神伝直心影流 classical sword tradition

kata 形 prearranged movement pattern

katana 刀 Japanese sword, worn cutting edge up

katchu bujutsu 甲冑武術 martial techniques done while wearing armor

katsu 活 resuscitation techniques

katsujinken 活人剣 life-giving sword

kazunuki 数抜き drawing and cutting 3,000, 10,000, or 30,000 times; special practice of Tatsumi-ryu

keiko shokon 稽古照今 reflect on the old to understand the new

kempo 拳法 fist method; unarmed sparring methods or systems

ken 懸 attack; fall upon

ken 剣 sword

kendo 剣道 way of the sword; modern martial art of Japanese fencing

kenjutsu 剣術 techniques of the sword; swordsmanship

keppan 血判 blood seal made with vow upon entering a ryu

kesagiri 袈裟切 diagonal cut

ki 気 vital energy

kiai 気合 focused shouts

kiaijutsu 気合術 techniques of kiai; methods of exerting one's will on others

kirigami menjo 切紙免状 classical license on a simple piece of folded Japanese paper

kishomon 起請文 vow on entering a classical tradition

kobo itchi 攻防一致 attack and defense as a continuum of response in combat

kobudo 古武道 classical martial ways

kobujutsu 古武術 classical martial arts

kodachi 小太刀 short sword

kogusoku 小具足 grappling, usually in armor

kohai 後輩 junior

kokoro 心 spirit, heart, or mind; also *shin*

koku 石 traditional Japanese weight measure; used to specify income

kokyu 呼吸 breath, breathing

koppo 骨法 unarmed grappling

koryu 古流 classical or old tradition

koryu budo 古流武道 classical martial ways

koryu bujutsu 古流武術 classical martial arts

koshi no mawari 腰の廻 grappling, usually in light armor

kowami 剛身 unarmed grappling

kuda yari 管槍 spear with a sleeve

kuden 口伝 oral teachings

kuji 九字 nine signs; mudra used in esoteric Buddhism

kumite 組手 freestyle sparring in karatedo

kumiuchi 組打 grappling

Kurama-ryu kenjutsu 鞍馬流剣術 classical sword tradition

kuzushi 崩 balance-breaking

kyuba no michi 弓馬の道 way of mounted archery, lit. bow and horse; old name for the warrior arts

kyudo 弓道 way of the bow; modern martial art of Japanese archery

kyusho 急所 vital point

M

majutsu 魔術 techniques of invisibility

makimono 巻物 scroll

Maniwa Nen-ryu 馬庭念流 classical sword tradition

manrikigusari 万力鎖 lit. ten thousand power chain; weighted chain

Marishiten 摩利支天 Buddhist warrior goddess

meijin 名人 sage; master; expert

menkyo 免許 license

menkyo kaiden 免許皆伝 license of complete transmission

mikkyo 密教 rituals of esoteric Buddhism

mokuroku 目録 lit. catalog of techniques; transmission scroll or license

monomi 物見 scouting techniques of the Tatsumi-ryu

Morishige-ryu hojutsu 森重流砲術 classical matchlock musketry tradition

mudansha 無段者 lit. non-graded, or below black belt level

muga 無我 egolessness or selflessness

mukei bunkazai 無形文化財 intangible cultural assets

munen muso 無念無想 non-ideational thought; lit. no desires, no thoughts

musha shugyo 武者修行 itinerant training in martial arts

mushin 無心 freedom from discriminative thinking

muso 夢想 dream-vision

muso shinden 夢想神伝 transmission of the dream-vision of the deity

N

nagamaki 長巻 Japanese glaive with a particularly large or heavy blade

nagareru 流れる to flow

naginata 薙刀 Japanese glaive

naginatajutsu 薙刀術 techniques of the glaive; glaive art

nanadan 七段 rank of 7th degree black belt; also *shichidan*

Nihon Kobudo Kyokai 日本古武道協会 Japanese Classical Martial Arts Association

Nihon Kobudo Shinkokai 日本古武道振興会 Society for the Promotion of the Japanese Classical Martial Arts

ninja 忍者 mercenary specialists in espionage

nitto 二刀 two swords

O

obi 帯 belt or sash

odachi 大太刀 long sword

okuden 奥伝 inner or hidden transmissions of a ryu

okugi 奥義 secret teachings or principles; also ogi

omote 表 front, obvious, overt; opposite of *ura*

ongyoho 隠行法 invisibility

Ono-ha Itto-ryu kenjutsu 小野派一刀流剣術 classical sword tradition

otome-ryu 御留流 official, sometimes secret, martial tradition of a clan or domain

Owari Kan-ryu sojutsu 尾張貫流槍術 classical tradition of spearsmanship of the Owari domain

R

randori 乱取 freestyle or sparring in judo

randori-ho 乱取法 methods of freestyle practice or sparring in judo

ronin 浪人 lit., wave man; warrior unattached to a domain

ryu 流 formalized martial tradition or school; used almost synonymously with ryugi, ryuha

ryugi 流儀 formalized martial tradition or school; used almost synonymously with ryu, ryuha

ryuha 流派 formalized martial tradition or school; used almost synonymously with ryu, ryugi

ryuha daihyo 流派代表 representative of the tradition

S

samurai 侍 Japanese warrior; see bushi

sansenjin 三戦神 three war kami; Fudo Myoo, Aizen Myoo, and Marishiten

saya 鞘 Japanese sword scabbard

seiryoku zenyo 精力善用 maximum efficient use of energy

seiza 正座 formal seated position

sempai 先輩 senior

sen no sen 先の先 taking the initiative; also *tai no tai*

sensei 先生 lit. one who was born before; teacher

sensen no sen 先々の先 pre-active, preemptive initiative; *kakari no sen*

shiai 試合 match, competition

shihan 師範 senior instructor

shihanke 師範家 master teacher

Shindo Munen-ryu kenjutsu
神道無念流劍術 classical sword tradition

Shingyoto-ryu kenjutsu 心形刀流劍術 classical sword tradition

Shinkage-ryu heiho 新陰流兵法 classical sword tradition

shinken 真劍 true or real sword; live blade

Shinmuso Hayashizaki-ryu battojutsu 神夢想林崎流抜刀術 classical tradition of sword-drawing

Shin no Shinto-ryu jujutsu 真之神道流柔術 classical jujutsu tradition

shinobi 忍び used to refer to agents of espionage

Shinto Muso-ryu jojutsu 神道夢想流杖術 classical jo tradition

shitsuke 躾 breeding or training

shizentai 自然体 natural body posture

shubaku 手搏 term for jujutsu

shudan sentoho 集団戦闘法 Tatsumi-ryu group-fighting tactics or methods

shugyo 修行 ascetic training

shuriken 手裏劍 throwing darts

shurikenjutsu 手裏劍術 techniques of throwing darts; throwing-blade art

siddhi [Sanskrit] supernatural powers of a Buddhist deity

sogo bujutsu 総合武術 integrated, composite martial arts/systems

sojutsu 槍術 techniques of the spear; spearsmanship

soke 宗家 headmaster

suhada bujutsu 素肌武術 martial techniques done in street clothes

suki 隙 opening

sumai no sechie 相撲の節会 ritual performances of sumo; Japanese traditional wrestling

T

tachi 太刀 Japanese sword; can be a general term or can refer to swords worn cutting edge down

tai 待 static or quiescent waiting

Takenouchi-ryu 竹内流 classical comprehensive martial tradition

tameshiai 試合 mutual testing; competing against one's own self

tankendo 短剣道 way of the short sword; modern adjunct art to jukendo

tanto 短刀 knife; dagger; dirk

tantra [Sanskrit] Buddhist ritual text focused on the cult of a deity

Tatsumi-ryu 立身流 classical comprehensive martial tradition

teki 敵 enemy

Tendo-ryu naginatajutsu 天道流薙刀術 classical school of naginata

tengu 天狗 long-nosed goblin; often associated with martial prowess

Tenjin Shinyo-ryu jujutsu 天神真楊流柔術 classical jujutsu tradition

Tenshin Shoden Katori Shinto-ryu 天真正伝香取神道流 classical comprehensive martial tradition

tessen 鉄扇 iron fan

tessenjutsu 鉄扇術 iron fan techniques; truncheon art using an iron fan

Toda-ha Buko-ryu naginatajutsu 戸田派武甲流薙刀術 classical *naginata* tradition

tode 捕手 term for unarmed grappling and arrest techniques; jujutsu

tojutsu 刀術 techniques of the sword; swordsmanship

tokonoma 床の間 decorative alcove

tori 取 lit., taker; the one who executes technique

torimi 取身 term for the one who takes or executes technique in Tenjin Shinyo-ryu

torite 取手 term for jujutsu and arrest techniques

U

uke 受 lit., receiver; the one on whom techniques are executed

ukemi 受身 lit., receiving; receiving techniques in kata; the one who receives a technique in Tenjin Shinyo-ryu

ura 裏 reverse, or back; opposite of omote

uwagi 上着 jacket worn for martial arts training

W

wakizashi 脇差 short sword

Y

Yagyu Shingan-ryu taijutsu 柳生心眼流体術 classical martial tradition centered on grappling

Yagyu Shinkage-ryu hyoho 柳生新陰流兵法 classical sword tradition

yari 槍 spear

yawara 柔 term for jujutsu

yawaragi 柔技 term for jujutsu

yoriki 与力 Tokugawa period law enforcement official

yoroi kumiuchi 鎧組打 battlefield grappling in armor

yoroidoshi 鎧通し dagger-like thrusting blade for use against armor

Yoshin-ryu jujutsu 楊心流柔術 classical jujutsu tradition

Yoshin-ryu naginatajutsu 楊心流薙刀術 classical tradition of naginata

yudansha 有段者 those holding black belt rank

yugamae 弓構 posture for shooting a bow

yumi 弓 bow; also refers to Japanese archery

Z

zanshin 残心 vigilance upon completion of technique

zubon ズボン trousers

INDEX

Index   185

Index 187

Index

Index   191